COMPUTERS
FOR
LIBRARIES

COMPUTERS FOR LIBRARIES

Second Edition

J E ROWLEY

CLIVE BINGLEY LONDON

First edition published 1980 by Clive Bingley Ltd.
First edition © 1980 J E Rowley

This second, revised edition, published 1985 by Clive Bingley Ltd,
The Library Association, 7 Ridgmount Street, London WC1E 7AE and
printed and bound in Great Britain for the publishers by Redwood
Burn Limited, Trowbridge, Wiltshire. Typesetting by Allset Composi-
tion, London. All rights reserved. No part of this publication may be
photocopied, recorded or otherwise reproduced, stored in a retrieval
system or transmitted in any form or by any electronic or mechanical
means without the prior permission of the publisher and copyright
holder.

Copyright © this edition J E Rowley
Reprinted 1986

British Library Cataloguing in Publication Data

Rowley, J. E.
    Computers for libraries.—2nd ed.
    1. Libraries—Automation
    I. Title
    025'.0028'54   Z678.9
    ISBN 0-85157-388-6

Contents

Acknowledgements

I should like to acknowledge all the support that I have received in writing this book. I am particularly indebted to the writers of previous literature, to the operators of systems that I have visited, and to those systems operators who have generously permitted me to use examples of their print-outs. They are too numerous to mention individually, but the source of each figure is given alongside the figure. I must also acknowledge my debt to my family for their continuing patience and support.

JER

Preface to second edition

In the five years since the first edition of this work was prepared, the impact of computers both in and on the library
and information world has been extensive, and has often
triggered fundamental changes. Perhaps one of the most
exciting features of the past five years is the extent to which
computers have begun to feature in an appropriate manner in
increasing numbers of libraries. There is now no area of
librarianship where computers cannot be used to good effect
to support the storage and exploitation of documents and
information. With the extension and diversification of the
application of computers in libraries it becomes ever more
important for all library and information workers to be
aware of the contribution that computers can make in
library and information work.

As the impact of computers spreads, so it becomes more
difficult to condense developments and practice into a brief
overview. Nevertheless, I still believe that such an overview,
for all its omissions and generalizations, can still play a useful
role. This second edition, then, although slightly expanded to
take account of new developments, is essentially an updating
of the first edition. The structure of the first edition has
largely been retained. This is especially evident in the separate
treatment given to different functions. Although many systems now integrate many functions, it is still useful to take
time to focus on each of these functions in turn.

Although changes are such that a fairly thorough review of
the text was necessary, it is surprising to see the same names,
systems and system functions persisting. This has much to do
with the character of developments in the past five years,
which have focussed on consolidation and integration, and
improvement of existing systems.

J E Rowley
November 1984

List of abbreviations

Note: This is a list of the more common abbreviations used in this text. On occasions it has proved difficult to discriminate between acronyms and abbreviations, but, in general, acronyms are not included. For information on acronyms the reader should consult the index under the appropriate acronym. Key databases, hosts, software packages and cooperatives are included, but the coverage in these areas is not comprehensive, since to produce such a complete list would take more space than such a list merits in this context.

AACR	Anglo-American cataloguing rules
AACR 2	Anglo-American cataloguing rules, second edition
ADP	Automatic Data Processing Inc.
AERE	Atomic Energy Research Establishment
AGRIS	Agricultural Information System
ALA	American Library Association
ALS	Automated Library Systems Ltd
ASSASSIN	Agricultural System for Storage and Subsequent Selection of Information
BCOP	Birmingham Libraries Cooperative
BELINDIS	Belgian Information and Dissemination Service
BIBDES	Bibliographic Data Entry System
BIOSIS	Biosciences Information
BL	British Library
BLAISE	British Library Automated Information Service
BLBSD	British Library Bibliographic Services Division

BLCMP	formerly Birmingham Libraries Cooperative Mechanization Project
BLLD	British Library Lending Division
BOSS	BLCMP Online Support Service
BRS	Bibliographic Retrieval Services Inc.
BSI	British Standards Institution
BTI	British Technology Index (now CTI)
CAG	Cooperative Automation Group
CAS	Chemical Abstracts Services
CIM	Computer input microform
CIP	Cataloguing-in-Publication
COM	Computer output microform
COMARC	Cooperative Machine-Readable Cataloguing
COMPENDEX	Computerized Engineering Index
CONSER	Conversion of Serials
COPOL	Council of Polytechnic Librarians
CPU	Central Processing Unit
CTI	Current Technology Index
DBMS	Database management system
DIANE	Direct Information Access Network for Europe
DIMDI	Deutsches Institut für medizinische Dokumentation und Information
DMS	Data management system
EDS	Exchangeable disk store
EI	Engineering Index
EMMA	Extra-MARC material
ERIC	Educational Resources Information Center
ES	Expert system
ESA	European Space Agency
ESRO	European Space Research Organization
EULOGIA	Edinburgh University Library Online for General Information Access
FDS	Fixed disk store
FID	Fédération Internationale de Documentation
FTX	Free text
HMSO	Her Majesty's Stationery Office
IBM	International Business Machines
ICL	International Computers Ltd
ICSU	International Conference of Scientific Unions

IFLA	International Federation of Library Associations
INIS	International Nuclear Information System
INSPEC	Information Service in Physics, Electrotechnology, and Computers and Control
IPSS	International Packet Switch Stream
IRRD	International Road Research Documentation Scheme
IRS	Information Retrieval Services of ESA
ISBD	International Standard Bibliographic Description
ISBD(G)	ISBD (General)
ISBD(S)	ISBD (Serials)
ISBN	International Standard Book Number
ISDS	International Serials Data System
ISI	Institute for Scientific Information
ISO	International Standards Organization
ISSN	International Standard Serial Number
KWAC	Keyword-and-Context
KWIC	Keyword-in-Context
KWIT	Keyword-in-Title
KWOC	Keyword-out-of-Context
LA	Library Association
LAN	Local Area Network
LASER	London and South-East Region
LC	Library of Congress
LIBRIS	Library Information System
LIS	Lockheed Information Systems
LOCAS	Local Catalogue Service
MARC	Machine-Readable Cataloguing
MARC(S)	Machine-Readable Cataloguing (serials)
MASS	MARC-based Automated Serials System
MEDLARS	Medical Literature Analysis and Retrieval System
MEDLINE	MEDLARS Online
MINICS	Minimal Input Cataloguing System
MULS	Minnesota Union List of Serials
MUMS	Multiple Use MARC System
NCC	National Computing Centre
NEMROC	Newcastle Media Resources Organization Committee
NSDC	National Serials Data Centre

NTIS	National Technical Information Service
NUC	National Union Catalog
OCLC	Online Computer Library Center
OCR	Optical character recognition
OS	Operating system
PEARL	Periodicals Enquiry Acquisition and Registration Locally
PRECIS	Preserved Context Indexing System
PSS	Packet Switch Stream
PTT	Postal, Telegraph and Telecommunications Authority
RAPRA	Rubber and Plastics Research Association
RECON	Retrospective Conversion
RLG	Research Libraries Group
RLIN	Research Libraries Information Network
SCOLCAP	Scottish Libraries Cooperative Automation Project
SCONUL	Standing Conference of National and University Libraries
SDC	Systems Development Corporation
SDI	Selective Dissemination of Information
SHE	Subject Headings for Engineering
SHEMROC	Sheffield Media Resources Organization Committee
SLIC	Selective Listing in Combination
SWALCAP	South-West Area Libraries Cooperative Automation Project
UBC	Universal Bibliographic Control
UKLDS	United Kingdom Library Database System
UNIBID	UNISIST International Centre for Bibliographic Description
UNIMARC	Universal MARC format
UNISIST	United Nations Information System in Science and Technology
UTLAS	University of Toronto Library Automation System
VDU	Visual display unit
WLN	Washington Library Network
WPI	World Patents Index

Chapter One

Introduction

The impact of computers, be they mainframe, mini or micro, has permeated all sectors of librarianship and information retrieval. The applications of computers in libraries can be grouped into those concerned with housekeeping routines and those directed towards information retrieval. Nevertheless, although this is the classification adopted in this work, the student is encouraged to regard the whole as an integrated area. With cooperative schemes and international networks, housekeeping and information-retrieval systems have an increasing amount in common.

Housekeeping applications of computers include aspects of serials control, circulation control, cataloguing, ordering and acquisitions, and the collection of management statistics. Since the sixties, much of the progress in these areas has centred on computer-based systems. In many areas greater standardization, efficiency, cooperation and improved services have been achieved as a result of computerization. Computers were first seen as particularly appropriate in those organizations or cooperatives whose number of transactions in any one of the housekeeping functions was large. The first systems were based upon mainframe computers. Over the past three to four years the increasing availability of microcomputer software and hardware has made it desirable for even the smallest library and information units to consider the application of computers. Hence computer-based housekeeping systems have been widely implemented.

The potential of the computer-based information-retrieval system should spark the imagination. Technology can realize the ultimate aim of the information-retrieval specialist which is to make information available to any person, when and where it is required. Unfortunately, the economics and the politics of the situation prevent this dream from becoming a reality, but significant progress is being made towards this ultimate aim. Enormous computer-based databases and databanks have been developed over the past few years. Some databases contain the same type of bibliographic and statistical information that librarians and information officers previously accessed with the aid of printed directories, lists, indexes and bibliographies. Computer-based information-retrieval systems offer more convenient, more flexible and more comprehensive retrieval than manual information-storage and retrieval systems. There are large internationally accessible databases and databanks. Inhouse systems, ranging in size from relatively large mainframe- or minicomputer-based systems, down to microcomputer-based systems are also widely used.

This work is an introduction to the computer and its applications, primarily for students of librarianship and information science. The book is a brief overview of a relatively wide area. Within this context, the principles of each topic are identified, and illustrated by a few case studies. It is hoped that this will be a sufficient grounding from which the student can progress to a more detailed understanding of current and future developments in this area. For the student who wishes to pursue the topic further, short, very selective, reading lists are given at the end of most chapters. These in themselves will often offer other readings for further study. The texts listed at the end of this chapter are particularly useful since they mostly present a further structured approach to the computerization of library processes.

However, care must be exercised in using any earlier texts. Accounts of computerization in libraries, like all other accounts of professional practice, are likely to become dated. To keep adequately informed it is important to peruse the periodical literature at regular intervals. Significant periodicals which cover computerization of library processes include:

Electronic library
Information technology and libraries
Program
Software review
Vine

A number of other periodicals concern themselves with aspects of computerized library and information activities as these are relevant to their coverage. Some of the more notable titles in this set are:

Aslib proceedings
Catalogue and index
The Indexer
International cataloguing
Journal of documentation
Journal of librarianship
Library acquisitions: practice and theory
Library resources and technical services
Online
Online review
Refer
Reference quarterly
Special libraries

Further, more specific information may be gleaned from systems operators and information service vendors. The student should make good use of the opportunities available to him to experience interaction with as many different computer-based library or information-retrieval systems as possible.

Why use a computer?

Subsequent chapters in this book will explain how to establish a computer-based library or information system, and show how the computer is used in various applications. But why do library and information system managers turn to computers? It is important to be able to give a clear answer to this question in order that the correct system is selected. Pressures towards computerization can generally be fitted into one of the following four categories:

a) *Increased workload:* An increased workload can arise from the need to control or access larger numbers of documents. This may be as a result of an overall increase in the number of documents published or the size of the library stock, or may derive from a need to cover a wider subject area. Increased workloads can also stem from a desire or necessity to provide a larger number of patrons with an adequate service. Computerization can be helpful in meeting increased workloads with a constant or decreasing staff.

b) *Need for greater efficiency:* Computerization may be viewed as a means of saving staff time and/or money. The records held in a computer may be more accurate, and more accessible than their manual equivalents. Work flow may be more rapid and more systematic.

c) *New services:* Computerization may offer the opportunity to offer services, in addition to existing services, at little extra cost. One of the main advantages of a computer-based system is the facility for re-arranging and selecting records to offer special listings. Examples of such services might be a union serials list, a current awareness service, and statistics for library decision-making.

d) *Cooperation and centralization:* The mere existence of another library which has made a success of a computerization programme is sufficient to attract interest. But the advantages of computerization can be more far-reaching. One element in many computerization programmes is the availability of external data which can be exploited to greater effect on a computer-based system. Centralized data and its availability is a significant factor in the move to computerized cataloguing systems. The ability to share records and some of the burdens of planning and designing a system has had a significant effect in most housekeeping operations. The amalgamation of public libraries in the United Kingdom particularly, was seen as an apt moment for computerization which would lead to a common system.

The above are reasons why libraries and information systems may be considered for computerization. It must, however, be emphasized that computerization will only relieve pressures on these services if an appropriate scheme is properly implemented. Inappropriate selection will at best increase pressure on workloads in the short term, and, at worst, lead to a frustrating period of unsuccessful implementation which may culminate in the selection of a further system, when the library has poorly ordered records and a disillusioned staff. Chapter two develops this topic further.

Finding computer equipment
Libraries and information units have a variety of arrangements for accessing computers and associated equipment. Some libraries buy or lease their own computer. This is

most likely to be a mini- or microcomputer which may be used alone or in conjunction with a larger computer. This option will be reviewed more fully in chapter three. A second possibility, often dictated by outside controls, is the use of an institutional computer. Many public, university and special libraries are constrained by economic or other factors to use the computer belonging to their parent body. The success of this approach depends on the quality of the communication between computer-centre staff and library staff and the facilities that the parent computer has to offer.

Other libraries and information units may opt for the processing facilities offered by a commercial computer bureau. Although this is usually more expensive than using an institutional computer, there is more freedom in the choice of an appropriate system. Commercial bureaux are primarily selling computer time, but may also offer systems and programming services.

A shared or cooperative facility may be the cheapest alternative. Cooperative systems usually acquire their own computer or computer network. Provided that the interests of the various parties in the cooperative do not conflict, this can be an effective solution, as the computer is devoted to library and information processing.

Whichever option is selected it is important to consider the following points:

a)   promptness of processing, ie online response times, or, with batch processing, turn-round times;

b)   reliability of equipment and maintenance arrangements;

c)   the balance of flexibility and stability in the manufacturer's range, ie both, are now models with enhanced features likely to become available and be compatible with older equipment, and, is older equipment likely to be supported by the manufacturer?

d)   the attitudes and provision of technical support staff;

e)   will the software which is required for the function to be achieved run on the equipment?

Whether or not the library or information unit is engaged in buying its own computer, it will generally have to acquire some terminal or other equipment for use in the library. Such equipment may be leased or bought; leasing is generally preferred, as new models can be obtained more easily, as they enter the market.

Sources of information on equipment include: computer yearbooks and publications, trade exhibitions, computer equipment manufacturers and their product literature, and the National Computing Centre in Manchester. Other advice can be obtained from consultants (at a price) or from other knowledgeable libraries, especially fellow cooperative members and from centres such as the Online Information Centre and the Catalogue Research Centre. The Library Technology Centre at the Polytechnic of Central London was established in 1982 with the aim of offering information, education and advice in the area of information technology in libraries. The following factors are important to ascertain in selecting equipment:

a) general description of system, including equipment and the software that it will support.

b) delivery schedules.

c) installation requirements on site, eg special issue counter, electrical power, air conditioning, security arrangements and lighting.

d) support to be provided by manufacturer, eg training.

e) financial aspects, eg rent, discounts.

f) maintenance and contracts.

g) expandability and compatibility with other and later, newer equipment.

Obviously the effective evaluation of the software to run on the machines is also important. This topic is considered in more detail later.

Further reading

Burton, P *Microcomputer applications in libraries and information retrieval: a directory of users.* Edinburgh, Leith Nautical College, 1981.

'Glossary'. *Vine* August 1979. 45-54.

Lundeen, G W and Davis, C H 'Library automation' in William, M E (ed) *Annual review of information science and technology*, vol 17. White Plains (New York), Knowledge Industry Publications, 1982. 161-86.

Paice, C D *Information retrieval and the computer.* London, Macdonald and Jane's, 1977.

Sager, D J *Public library administrators' planning guide to automation.* Dublin (Ohio), OCLC, 1983. (OCLC library, information and computer science series, 2)

Salmon, S R *Library automation systems.* New York, Marcel Dekker, 1975.

Tedd, L A *An introduction to computer based library systems.* 2nd ed. Chichester, Wiley, 1984.

Tedd, L A 'Report on a visit to European computer-based information centres'. *Program* 13(2) April 1979. 47-57.

Williams, H L (ed) *Computerised systems in library and information services.* London, Aslib, 1983.

Wilson, C W J *Directory of operational computer applications in United Kingdom libraries and information units.* 2nd ed. London, Aslib, 1977.

Woods, R G *Library automation.* (BL Research Reviews, 2) BL, July 1982.

Gillman, P and Peniston, S *Library automation: a current review.* London, Unilever/Aslib, 1984.

Chapter Two

Planning and designing the computerized library system

A computerization programme for a library or set of library operations is a significant project. Before any system is installed a formal study will usually be undertaken to investigate the nature and potential of any new system. It is important to recognize that computerizing library data processing is akin to the development of a total information-management system for a company. Computerization will affect the basic records of the library and information service. Changes in cataloguing, indexing, acquisitions and circulation records can affect the character of library services. Thus, careful management of any mechanization programme is of vital importance. An organized systems-analysis exercise will contribute to successful implementation.

In some circumstances, the librarian is not engaged in designing a system, but rather in selecting the most appropriate system or package. In information-retrieval applications, for example, the librarian has to choose from a variety of established external systems. Increasingly, the librarian will not be involved in initial computerization, but rather in conversion from one computerized system to a more efficient or all-embracing system. The steps of a systems-analysis exercise still represent a useful structure, although the project may be easier to control, involving fewer people and a smaller expenditure.

The first step in conducting a systems-analysis exercise is to enlist the services of a systems analyst or a systems-analysis team. A systems analyst can take a more impartial view of the library system than might a librarian. He provides the interface between the librarian and the data-processing staff and analyses the librarian's requirements in relation to the computer's capabilities. Nevertheless, all senior library staff are likely to be engaged to some extent in the systems-analysis exercise, and it will greatly enhance the ease and success of the enterprise if the library staff understand the procedure. The librarian needs to be able to talk to the computer and systems-analysis staff in their own terms. This account will give a simple introduction to the main stages in a systems-analysis exercise.

Although systems-analysis strategies vary, the following six main steps are likely to be encountered in most systems-analysis exercises:

a) definition of objectives,   d) design phase,
b) feasibility study,   e) implementation phase,
c) definition phase,   f) evaluation.

None of these stages is self-contained or rigidly delimited. The design, definition and implementation phases will all reconsider aspects of the system, that have been studied in less depth during an earlier stage. Similarly, it may be neccessary, after work has started in the design phase, to supplement work conducted in the definition phase. 'Back-tracking' is inevitable.

Nevertheless, to view the exercise as comprising six steps aids the beginner, and facilitates communication within a team. Clearly defined stages help in the allocation of tasks and the setting of deadlines. A plan makes it easier to evaluate progress and individual workloads, and may be presented to, and agreed by, the parent authority.

A preliminary stage is to establish a steering committee, who will initiate the systems-analysis exercise and supervise the project. This committee is best comprised of persons from all levels in the library operations, but must include top management with the power to implement decisions.

Plainly, if the first three stages lead to a conclusion that a ready-made package or system including both software and hardware, or participation in a cooperative or international network is the most desirable option, then there will be no need for many of the design steps in stage four to be fully explored. Nevertheless, even here design is necessary, although it may be chiefly addressed to fitting an off-the-peg system to a specific library's requirements. Equally, whether a new system is designed from the beginning or an established system is taken and adapted, careful implementation and evaluation remain important.

It is important to remember that many libraries may conduct several systems-analysis exercises, or parts thereof, at different points in time, and in relation to different areas of activity. Obviously a relatively all-embracing analysis of the library's operations helps the entire range of library operations to be viewed as a whole, and increases the likelihood of the various subsystems which perform different functions being compatible with one another. Unfortunately, such an extensive systems-analysis exercise may not be always possible, or even viewed as desirable. A number of personnel, economic and social factors may militate against a complete analysis of all operations. Nevertheless, it must always be recognized that the choice and implementation of a package is time-consuming, and time must be allocated for this activity even if a relatively cheap package is selected.

a) Definition of objectives

When a librarian first entertains the idea of computerization, this is usually in response to some inadequacy in the extant situation. This might include demands for change from governing bodies or users, or increasing backlogs due to shortage of staff, budget or space. The librarian may be faced with establishing a new information centre or library, but it is more likely that there is an existing facility based on manual procedures. The first step is to review established library policies and practices. The objectives of the computerization project must be clearly defined in the wider context of the library's overall objectives. Which services should the library be providing and which of these will it be in a position to offer to the required standards during the next few years? Future as well as current objectives must be considered.

Some of the pressures that precede computerization are reviewed in general terms in chapter one. These will be further elucidated in subsequent chapters. The objectives of the computerization programme must encompass plans to relieve such pressures. Objectives for library computerization are often developed in terms of a planned progression of systems, starting with a simple improvement and moving, step by step, to the ultimate, more sophisticated system. Alternatively, if a library or cooperative is engaged in transferring from one system to another it is sound practice to transfer one set of operations, say, those associated with circulation control, before transferring other operations, such as those related to acquisitions control and cataloguing. For example, online circulation control may be available to library staff some months before online public access catalogues are made available for the public to consult, despite both functions being features of the same system. Thus, general objectives can be tested before over-commitment to a particular course of action. Also, an operational system, if only a partial system, is guaranteed, even if projected funding is not forthcoming, and will not, in the event, stretch to the planned sophisticated version.

The objectives must identify which functions will be affected by the system, eg cataloguing and information services. Some functions will continue as previously, others will experience a significant change which might affect both staff and users (as in the change from microfilm to online public-access catalogues), and yet others will represent new services such as local text-retrieval databases and systems.

Having ensured that there is a problem awaiting solution it is safe to proceed to the feasibility study.

b) Feasibility study
The aim of the feasibility study is to complete a report summarizing the possible ways of accomplishing the project objectives, in the light of the costs and benefits of each approach. Such a report will normally recommend a preferred approach. The feasibility study environment enables all alternatives to be dispassionately discussed and evaluated.

This phase starts with an identification of the main characteristics of the required system. The level of analysis of the library's proposed operating system is only that absolutely necessary for cost estimation and preliminary planning. The constraints on the new system such as timing, financial, staffing or political need to be identified. A useful means of encouraging thoroughness is to apply the interrogatives, What, Why, When, Who and Where, to each element of all proposed and established systems. These interrogatives can fruitfully be levelled at any existing system, manual or computerized, even if as a result the plan for change proceeds no further. Care must be taken to avoid change for change's sake, or because the salesman would like to make a healthy commission by selling his latest system. New systems and features should only be selected if they offer real advantages or benefits.

At the same time as examining the local environment it is worthwhile to learn something of the activities of other libraries. In particular, inspection of other existing systems may lead to the selection of a package system, or participation in a network, either during this or the next phase.

During this stage it is important to collect as much information as possible about the software packages that might meet the specification, from as many sources as possible. Obviously the software houses and other suppliers of the packages are important. So too are directories, periodicals which review software packages and other accounts of the software packages and their possible implementation. Workshops, exhibitions and conferences offered by professional associations, library schools and other groups may be valuable, and certainly much can be gleaned from direct contact with users of any software packages under consideration. A reputable software vendor should be willing to put a potential purchaser in contact with other users. Obviously this stage will result in a large collection of information. Certainly it will provide useful education concerning the range of possible options.

Normally, the central endeavour of a feasibility study is a cost-benefit analysis of the various alternatives. A full cost-benefit analysis is unlikely to be appropriate in a library situation, particularly when the system under analysis has not yet been instituted. But a partial analysis can almost always be conducted, and even this process may yield useful insights.

Cost-benefit analysis can be defined as a systematic comparison between the cost of carrying out a service or activity, and the value of that service or activity, qualified as far as possible, all cost and benefits (direct and indirect, financial and social) being taken into account. Cost-benefit analysis involves the listing and consideration of as many effects as can be identified, beneficial and adverse, short-term, long-term, tangible and intangible, on all persons or groups likely to be affected by a proposed project or service.

Even in the best circumstances it is extremely difficult to conduct a full cost-benefit analysis. In a library or information system the main problem is the intangible nature of most of the benefits. Some direct savings should be identifiable, such as reduction in clerical personnel's effort, elimination of postage, improved procedures, greater security etc. These direct savings are, with a little ingenuity, calculable; but they can be small compared with the total incurred cost of the new system. In addition, complex discounting of future benefits and costs may be necessary in order to complete the exercise. This is yet more difficult to perform meaningfully. The main benefits are qualitative rather than quantitive. Benefits might include an improved overall performance, more and better services to users, more management information or a more flexible system with potential for extension and modification. Parameters that might contribute to a study of benefits might be willingness to pay (of, say, users or management, eg company or local authority), or time saved for staff or users of the information unit, or the cost of an alternative method. This last parameter is particularly likely to be useful in assessing a number of options offered by the different systems suppliers.

Cost-effectiveness analysis is a more straightforward technique which is often used in a library and information-system study. Cost-effectiveness analysis is a method of finding either the cheapest means of accomplishing a defined objective or the maximum value from a given expenditure. A cost-effectiveness study will involve a detailed analysis of an existing library or information system in terms of the activities performed and the personnel who are responsible for completing them. Hypotheses must then be made about the effects of modifying the system, and an analysis of the alternative system conducted. The costs and effectiveness of two or more systems are then compared.

It will be easier to understand what a cost-effectiveness analysis involves if one has a clear view of the costs incurred during computerization. Costs associated with a computerization programme can be divided into the following four groups, each of which contains both set-up and ongoing elements:

a) *systems personnel costs,* including costs of time for systems design, programming and program testing;

b) *library personnel costs,* including costs of time for participation in systems design, study, training and establishing new procedures and maintenance. Conversion of files can be a major element in cost; existing borrower and book files are expensive to check and convert, unless the two systems are compatible;

    c) *equipment costs*, including costs for computer time and other computer-associated equipment, and costs for library equipment, eg microfilm readers, terminals; and the more minor

    d) *material costs*, relating, for instance, to paper or forms.

Costs incurred during the inauguration of a system will vary over a period of time, peaking during the implementation phase. With successful completion of implementation most development costs will have been incurred and any continuing costs will arise from operation and maintenance until, of course, the need for system enhancement becomes apparent in years to come. The ongoing costs can be expected to include costs for: equipment (replacement and enhancement), operating personnel for equipment (which may be available within the library's organization, but at a cost for which it is difficult to provide a figure), library personnel and supplies. Both the scale and relative magnitude of these costs will depend on the system and its functions.

With an array of cost data, costs and benefits are compared within a relevant framework. For example, cumulative costs, including development and operating costs, may be taken into account, or development costs may have been met by a special funding arrangement, and operating costs alone will be of continuing concern. Any benefits or costs which are deferred must be regarded as being of less value than their immediate counterparts, although a precise estimate of future costs and benefits may be elusive.

At the end of the feasibility study a report is presented to library management, for their support in proceeding to the next stages.

c) Definition phase

The definition phase is directed towards compiling a system definition, which will, if acceptable, be implemented in the subsequent design phase. Each aspect of the system that was examined in the feasibility stage must be analysed at much greater length.

A re-evaluation of the objectives of the current system, and the extent to which the system meets these objectives is the first task. Objectives can be defined on several levels and, indeed, should first be defined at a general level, then systematically reduced to more specific statements. For example, at a general level the object of a current awareness service might be to keep users aware of new developments. Stated more explicitly this could be interpreted as:

a) to reduce duplication in research and development;

b) to reduce by twenty-five per cent the amount of time that a researcher spends in searching current literature; or,

c) to alert staff to conferences of potential interest.

A system definition for a library computerized system will describe the library's system requirements in detail, giving:

a) details of the frequency of operation of the system;

b) details of machine time and programming effort;

c) details of the production of any master files;

d) input requirements and procedures;

e) proposals for the processing and output of records;

f) an overall summary of the system.

The system definition will often be augmented by a plan for the subsequent stages of the project. At this stage the system definition should be studied for compatibility with other library projects and be presented to library policy-makers for their approval.

d) Design phase

During the design phase, a detailed design for both the computer system and the library personnel is drafted. This phase results in documents that detail the functions to be programmed and the operating procedures to be adopted by personnel. Tasks typical of the design phase are:

a) Describe the physical and administrative organization of the library with the aid of organization charts, policy manuals, personnel descriptions, etc.

b) Conduct a detailed examination of the flow of work, using flowcharts, decision tables, etc. Flowcharting is a valuable tool for pinpointing the main entities and activities in a system. Figure 2.1 shows the main flowcharting symbols, and figure 2.2 depicts a systems-analysis exercise in flowchart format.

c) Finalize processing, output requirements and data relationships, and interpret these in terms of specific equipment, operating environments and response times.

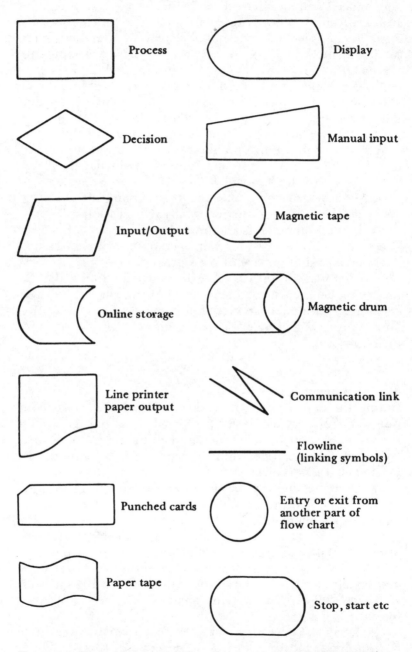

Process

Display

Decision

Manual input

Input/Output

Magnetic tape

Online storage

Magnetic drum

Line printer
paper output

Communication link

Flowline
(linking symbols)

Punched cards

Entry or exit from
another part of
flow chart

Paper tape

Stop, start etc

Figure 2.1: Flowchart symbols (in accordance with BS 4058: 1973)

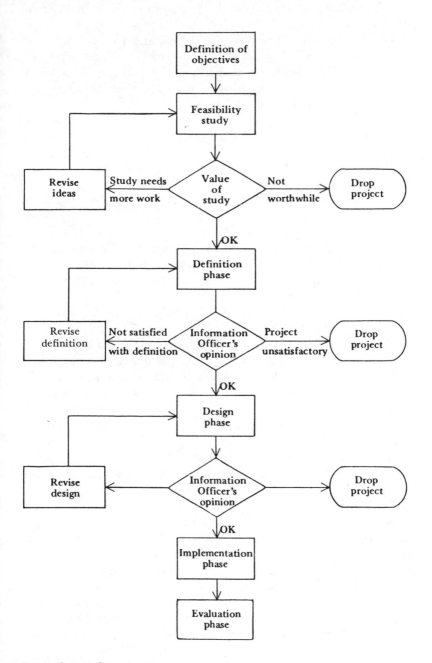

Figure 2.2: A flowchart

  d) Collect data on file sizes, amounts of activity, processing times and costs.

  e) Design the formats and organization of all files and forms, including computer-stored records.

  f) Specify the logical manipulations and transformations within each part of the library function that are to be performed by the computer.

  g) Develop requirements for editing, formatting, storing and updating of machine-stored data, and establish control procedures.

  h) Identify and prepare specifications for programs and manual procedures.

  i) Submit revised estimates of the operational costs of the system.

  j) Plan the subsequent phases.

At some stage during the design phase it will be necessary to select equipment and place orders. Some introductory remarks on equipment selection are to be found in chapter three.

e) Implementation phase

All planning has now been completed and the transformation to a fully operational system can commence. The first jobs will be the writing, debugging and documenting of all computer programs and their integration into a total system. The establishment of master files will take place next. Programming is complete when programs have been demonstrated to library management and they are satisfied that the programs conform to the detailed specification.

  When the system is ready for implementation, emphasis switches to communication with library staff and users. Open discussion with staff is important from the beginning of the project. Staff can be expected to be concerned about the effect of the new system on their jobs, and may react negatively to change. During the implementation phase, it is important that all staff concerned be apprised of the objectives and overall operation of the system. They will need training in how the new system will change the detailed performance of their duties, and need to understand how their role relates to the system as a whole. An organized training programme is advisable, and this can include visits, seminars, conferences, demonstrations, newsletters, courses, etc.

One member of staff, who understands the system and, to some extent, the equipment, should be made responsible for the smooth operation of the system. He can coordinate various aspects of the implementation and diagnose malfunctions.

Users also need to be informed about those aspects of the new system that will affect them. The exploration of an online catalogue can be an exciting or an embarrassing experience, depending on the adequacy of documentation and explanation and the availability of help facilities. New services, such as online retrospective searching or current awareness bulletins which have recently become available through, say, a research establishment's computer at any terminal on the site, must be advertised when the time is ripe.

Existing files such as catalogues, serials records, borrower records and personnel files must all be converted from their present form. Since many of these files are very large, conversion of retrospective files may continue long after a system based on current files has been implemented. Arrangements for parallel use of retrospective files and current files must be settled.

The system may come into full operation via a number of possible routes. Complete changeover at one point in time is conceptually the most tidy. But this approach requires careful planning and coordination, particularly during the changeover. A phased approach, possibly implementing the section of the system relating to one operation or procedure (eg circulation control) first, and progressing to more novel or complex subsystems in the fullness of time, is likely to be less traumatic. A phased approach gives the staff time to adjust to the new system, but depends upon being able to split the system in discrete units. Another possibility — parallel running of the old and the new system — may provide a thorough check on the new system, without reliance on it. This approach is sensible where the consequences of failure are disastrous, but will require extra staff time. The fourth approach, pilot operation, permits any problem to be tackled on a smaller-scale operation. Pilot operation generally means the implementation of the complete system but at one location or branch only. Obviously, within a cooperative or large library system various combinations of these implementation approaches may be tried.

f) Evaluation

Once the system has been running for a time, the extent to which the system is meeting its stated objectives should be reviewed. Often very small alterations in procedures or file organization may be repaid by significant improvements in efficiency. A maintenance plan which encourages ongoing communication between library staff and systems analysts or suppliers will facilitate modifications in the system as the library environment changes.

If a large library system undergoes systems analysis, effort will normally be directed towards one subsystem at a time, eg cataloguing, serials control, etc. Under such circumstances it is useful to have a chart of the work to be completed in each function and to link the completion of the different phases to the financial control of the library. A system may be divided into subsystems by function, subject, material, location or objectives.

Further reading

Boss, R W *The library manager's guide to automation.* White Plains (New York), Knowledge Industry Publications, 1979.

Daniels, A and Yeates, D *Basic systems analysis* London, Pitman, 1982.

Daniels, A and Yeates, D *Basic training in systems analysis.* 2nd ed. by D Yeates. London, Pitman, 1971.

Gates, H 'Factors to consider in choosing a microcomputer for library housekeeping and information retrieval in a small library: experience in the Cairns library'. *Program* 18(2) April 1984. 111-23

Hymans, M 'Tendering - the suppliers' viewpoint'. *Program* 13(4) October 1979. 169-76.

Lancaster, F W 'Systems design and analysis for libraries' *Library Trends* 21, 1973. 463-612.

Lee, B *Basic systems analysis.* London, Input Two-Nine, 1980. (Modular computer studies series, study unit G1).

Leimkuhler, F F 'The practice of operations research in libraries'. *Collection Management* 3 (2/3) Summer/Fall 1979. 127-38.

Library Association *The impact of new technology on libraries and information centres.* London, LA, 1983.

Matthews, J R *Choosing an automated library system: a planning guide.* Chicago, ALA, 1980.

Townley, H M *Systems analysis for information retrieval.* London, Deutsch, 1978.

Vickers, P H *Automation guidelines for public libraries.* London, HMSO, 1975.

Wainwright, J, 'Negotiating for a contract-drawing up the technical specification'. *Program* 13(4) October 1979. 158-64.

Chapter Three

Computers

One of the most difficult aspects of understanding computer-ized systems is unravelling the jargon. The wide variety of terminology is aggravated by the imprecise use of terms and changes in their use as technology advances. This chapter introduces the basic computer configuration and some of its modes of use.

Most librarians need only a passing acquaintance with the elements of computer processing. Many librarians resort to the computer chiefly as a filing, selection and re-formatting device, which should, if properly applied, eliminate much clerical slog. But it is imperative that the librarian under-stands sufficient computing terminology to communicate with computer systems experts and to evaluate systems for their effectiveness in a specific environment. Input and output devices are most likely to intrude into the library environment and hence they are dealt with in greater depth. This chapter establishes a structure for understanding the basic components of a computer configuration.

Computer system design is constrained by the machinery around which it has been planned and the librarian needs to appreciate this. However, there are systems which are too integrally dependent upon one particular equipment config-uration. Whilst all systems work more efficiently on some equipment than others, it is generally worth sacrificing some efficiency in a specific machine environment in favour of future flexibility. Computer hardware markets are extremely competitive, with new equipment continually entering the marketplace, and a library should be in a position to exploit new technology. For similar reasons, it is advisable to con-sider renting any in-library equipment, so that sophisticated models can be considered and installed as they become available.

The basic computer configuration

Any computer system can be said to encompass four activities: capture data at source, ie record data; prepare data in a form acceptable to a computer; perform processing requirements; communicate results of processing. The first two activities may be concurrent, as when an online terminal is used by a cataloguer for online cataloguing; cataloguing and data inputting are simultaneous. The following is a standard configuration for completing these four activites.

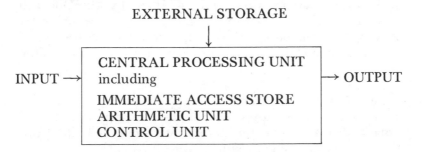

Figure 3.1: A basic computer configuration

Thus a computer comprises four main components: central processing unit, external or backing stores, and input and output devices.

The Central Processing Unit or CPU comprises the main (immediate access) store, the arithmetic unit and the control unit. The main store holds the information currently being processed. The store is made of devices capable of taking two possible states, one of which represents a '0' and the other a '1'. These bits of information can be grouped to form a byte (or character) and further grouped to form a word. The size of a computer is normally stated in terms of the main store size.

Data held in the immediate access store can be accessed almost instantaneously. The operating system, together with crucial programs, are held in the immediate access store. As data undergoes processing, it is temporarily held in the immediate access store. If the immediate access store is sufficiently large, several programs can be run simultaneously. The simultaneous processing of several programs, known as multiprogramming, is a means of making full use of the central processor time, in spite of the slower speeds of most input and output devices. Multiprogramming causes the computer to execute some commands from one program, some from another, and then to return to the first program. A priority system is normally part of the machine control program.

The arithmetic unit performs arithmetic operations and logical comparisons on the data held in the immediate access store.

The control unit exercises control over the operation of the arithmetic unit, the immediate access store and the input and output devices. Control is achieved by the Operating System (or OS), a master program. The operating system is usually supplied by the computer manufacturer and is designed to make the most efficient use of the computer's facilities.

External or auxiliary stores

Immediate access stores have a limited capacity and are volatile. Thus, most computer systems hold the bulk of their data on an external or auxiliary store.

Magnetic tape is a plastic tape, coated with ferrous oxide and similar in appearance to audio tape. Data is encoded in rows of seven or nine magnetic spots. Such codings are not universal and it may be necessary to convert a tape into a form compatible with a given magnetic tape-reader. Data may be written, read, erased and over-written by read-write heads which change or sense the magnetization of the spots. Tapes can be eradicated and re-used, and can be expected to store data for some time. Magnetic tape is coded with a magnetic-tape typewriter or encoder. Keyboard-to-tape units can be used in a stand-alone mode connected to a computer, or several keyboards may be linked to a minicomputer which controls editing, formatting and merging centrally.

As a store, magnetic tape offers sequential access. In other words, the read head must pass over a tape in order, until the sought item is located. All two thousand feet of a tape may have to be scanned and wound before a search is complete. Sequential access means slow and expensive sorting, merging and correcting of records stored on tape. Hence magnetic tapes tend to be used in batch mode operation, for instance to accumulate transactions, sort them, and process modified records. In order to reduce repetitive remerging of tapes, related data may be stored in several distinct locations on the tape, these locations being linked by addressing. In their favour, tapes store large quantities of data cheaply and are very portable; machine readable databases are often marketed on tape. Magnetic tape cassettes are more portable than tapes on spools.

Microcomputers use ordinary audio-cassettes with magnetic tape as storage devices. A unit must be present in any system which uses magnetic tape to read and write onto magnetic tape. With microcomputers this can be an ordinary audio cassette recorder.

A magnetic disk is a rotating circular plate, which is coated on both sides with a magnetizable substance. Data is represented by magnetically polarised spots arranged in concentric tracks. Disks are mounted on a central spindle to form a disk pack. Disk packs can be mounted permanently, known as fixed disk store (FDS), or can be removable, known as exchangeable disk store (EDS). Read-write heads can be directed to the opposite track, and then this track can be searched sequentially; a disk pack is a random-access device.

Floppy disks are used with smaller microcomputers; these are available in either 3½, 5¼ or 8 inch diameter sizes. Winchester disk drives allow hard disks to be run in conjunction with the more powerful microcomputers, and enhance the storage capacity of the auxiliary storage devices that may be used with microcomputers.

Although magnetic tapes and disks are the most common forms of backing store, other devices such as magnetic drums and cards have been tried, and new developments are in the pipeline. Two devices with potential are the charge-coupled device and magnetic bubbles. Experiments for the storage of digital information, as well as pictorial information on optical disks, are under way. The Library of Congress is using optical disks for storage of information and Derwent's VideoPat-Search makes use of this technology.

Here is a checklist of selection criteria for storage media and memory devices:

a) Physical nature of storage medium;

b) Functional features, eg ease of erasing, availability of direct access;

   c)   Quantitive characteristics, eg access time, data capacity, data transfer rate (for data from store to computer);
   d)   Methods of file organization,
   e)   Costs.
Plainly, different storage media will be appropriate in different applications.

Input devices
Input and output devices, together with auxiliary memory, are referred to as peripherals. Peripherals are slower in operation than the CPU. Slow speed peripherals are interfaced with the CPU by the intervention of buffer stores that hold data until the input of data for one job is complete and ready for the CPU's attention. Input devices are the means of transferring both instructions and data into computer systems, and generally involve coding characters into series of binary digits or bits.

   Punched cards are an established input medium; holes are punched in the body of the card in rows and columns to represent characters. The characters are often typed along the top of the card. Cards are prepared by a card punch, and read into the computer store via a card reader. Smaller and cheaper micro-punched cards are also marketed. Punched cards can be easily checked and amended, and are particularly suited to bibliographic data which is recorded in fixed fields, eg ISBN and other accession numbers.

   Paper tape is a strip of paper on which each character is represented by a unique pattern of holes, one character per row of five, six, seven or eight hole positions. Tape is punched, simultaneously with the typing of a hard-copy version, on a tape typewriter. Since tape feeds continuously it can be read more rapidly than cards, but correction demands either re-punching of the entire tape or splicing in corrected sections of tape. Both cards and tape will tolerate dispatch through the postal system or via other commercial carriers.

   There are a number of input devices where data is transferred direct to a computer store. Such online access for inputting data is the norm in systems being designed and implemented today. Sometimes access is to part of the database, but often the complete database can be accessed by an authorized user. With the aid of a terminal, a VDU and/or a printer, and a keyboard, records may be summoned, viewed, and amended. Terminals and networks are considered more fully in the remainder of this chapter. The key-to-tape units mentioned in the 'External or auxiliary stores' section (p. 24) fall into this category. The operator types material into a buffer or small store, and when the record is complete the data is transmitted to a magnetic tape or disk. Correction is as straightforward as with a typewriter. The light-pen is another data collection device. Used in the circulation system of a library, it usually reads data from a special label attached to each book, and transmits the data to a store. Other readers may sense cards marked with graphite pencils.

Magnetic ink character recognition is a means of deciphering characters printed in an ink containing magnetizable material. Before reading, the document is passed under a device which creates a magnetic field; these magnetizations are then detected by the reader. Characters used must be in a special format, as in cheque symbols. Optical character recognition again recognizes characters, but this time optically. The reader scans the document for reflected light patterns, and provided a recognized type font is used, translates the patterns into a time pattern of electrical signals which are passed to the computer store. Material may need to be converted into the special type font prior to OCR reading, and hence OCR often functions as an intermediary. Computer Input Microform (CIM) also makes it possible to input information directly from microfilm, but again depends usually on a select range of type fonts. Speech input is also possible, but systems are still in their infancy.

Output devices
Many peripherals function in both the input and output modes; these are described here together with pure output devices.

A line or impact printer prints a line of characters at a time, and is the main means of obtaining printed output. There are many models; chain, train, band and belt, all describe line printers. In such printers all identical characters on a line are printed simultaneously, eg all A's, then all B's, etc. The type characters are carried on an endless bar or chain and pass in front of a row of print hammers which strike the appropriate characters as they pass. Higher speeds and better quality can be achieved with more expensive equipment. Non-impact printers use electrical or electrostatic mechanisms which are faster. Laser printers are found in some applications; these give faster and higher quality printing. Laser printers are generally too expensive for the individual library to purchase and are therefore used on a bureaux basis. Daisy-wheel printers are used in smaller computer systems. Here the characters are mounted upon a daisy-like structure, and the wheels are interchangeable so that different type fonts may be used. These printers print one character at a time, at typical speeds of 30 or 80 characters per second (cps). Most printers use continuous stationery and upper case characters. Multi-part stationery, with interleaved carbon paper may provide up to six copies, and other types of paper permit other formats.

A visual display unit or VDU is a cathode ray tube, like a television, augmented by a typewriter keyboard, which is a means of two-way communication with the CPU. Each terminal requires a control unit with a buffer memory, which retains the input instructions until they are complete and then forwards them to the computer. VDUs are easy to read and use for long periods, fast and silent in use; but no permanent record is made, and long displays may disappear off the top of the screen and need to be recalled. The display on a VDU should have adequate contrast, be sharp and stable and large enough to contain a complete record. Cursors, which act as tabs on the screen, should be moveable to any position on the screen to facilitate flexibility in formatting. Intelligent terminals are considered in subsequent sections.

An alternative to the VDU in many applications is a printer or teleprinter, which is effectively a typewriter driven by the computer. Like the VDU it is usually accompanied by a keyboard for inputting, and thus permits two-way communication. A permanent record is produced of each search and some printers produce a very acceptable product. Printers that operate at faster speeds are more expensive.

Computer typesetting is used in a similar environment to line print-out, but the hard copy is of a better quality. Information from the computer is converted into fully made up pages in photographic film. This film constitutes the basis of printing plates for offset litho printing. Computer Output Microform (COM) equipment transfers data direct from the computer store to a microfilm or microfiche. COM can be

used to create plates for offset litho printing and is an economic proposition for printing large files of data, producing
very much less bulky output at faster speeds. COM films are
often generated from in-house magnetic tapes by bureaux
with the appropriate equipment.

Card punches and paper tape punches can be used to transfer information from the computer store onto cards or tape,
but this process is slow. The operator's console is a visual
display unit through which the operator can contact some of
the programs in the Operating System in order to ascertain
which programs are being processed, and load and unload
programs. The OS can also send messages to the operator
concerning necessary tasks such as loading and unloading files.
Graph plotters and the graphical display units offer special
facilities for the graphical display of information. Speech
synthesizers are a further possibility.

Here is a checklist of criteria for selection of input and
output modes:

a) Character set;
b) Size and nature of data input;
c) Means of checking during data input;
d) Compatibility of input and output equipment with
other computer equipment;
e) Cost;
f) Quality and form of output;
g) Quantity of output per copy;
h) Frequency and volume of output;
i) Speed of turn-round.

Computer Processing

Operation of a computer system may be batch or real-time.

Batch processing is becoming less common as the inherent
delays are regarded as particularly detrimental. In batch processing data is collected in batches, and then the supervisory
program determines the most economic time at which to
process it. Batch processing is particularly suitable where
regular runs are required, but may have serious drawbacks for,
for instance, a charging system when it is important to be able
to determine instantly who has borrowed which books. With
batch processing, typically, a print-out is produced which
enables the state of the files, say, of current items on loan

from a library, to be viewed as they were at the point in time when the last batch of records of loans was submitted for input to the computer database, the file was amended, and the print-out was taken from the amended file. Thus, normally, an overnight computer run will enable a print-out to show the state of items with regard to their loan status on the previous day; the present day's transactions will not be recorded. The advantage of this arrangement over online access to current files is that each service point does not need direct access to the files or to the computer. For a service point where the volume of transactions is low, batch processing might remain a sensible option.

In real-time systems, the processing of information is undertaken as the information enters the system. Real-time systems are the type normally used in conjunction with on-line operation and interactive terminals, as discussed below.

Remote-entry job processing has elements of online and batch processing. An online terminal is used to enter a job into the queue of jobs to be batch processed by the computer. This method benefits from the interactive capabilities of the online terminal, whilst taking advantage of cheap processing time.

Most larger computers operate on a time-sharing basis, where data from several input devices is apparently processed simultaneously. Even where there are several terminals connected to one computer, each terminal user may proceed as if he were the sole user. He has no means of detecting that the computer's attention is also being diverted to other jobs. The organization for these integrated activities is controlled by a supervisory program.

The term interactive processing may either be applied to situations where facilities are dynamically updated at the time the operator is keying in the data, or to situations where the file can be interrogated instantly, but not necessarily modified.

Multi-processing refers to the situation where a number of computers are linked to each other. Several smaller computers, often micro- or minicomputers, may perform more simple processing independently, but rely on a large computer for more complex jobs.

Networks

Networks are used for communication between a number of computers and between terminals and a computer. The network is a telecommunications network, which is linked via modems or acoustic couplers to the main computer and, at the other end, the terminal.

Almost any device that is capable of transmitting or receiving information may be regarded as a terminal. Terminals can be remote, ie remote from the main computer installation, and may be batch or interactive.

Batch terminals allow large volumes of batch processing to be achieved, possibly at a distance from the central computer facility. A simple remote batch terminal might consist of a card reader and a line printer, coordinated by a control unit. A more typical terminal might encompass a paper tape reader, paper tape punch, operator's console, line printer and card reader, all supervised by a control unit.

Interactive terminals are now much more common and permit the keying in of data, the data's transmission to the control computer and, within seconds, a computer response to the data received. A typical interactive terminal comprises either a VDU and its accompanying keyboard, and/or a printer. Remote VDU terminals may be connected to the computer in a variety of fashions. Figure 3.2 demonstrates some of these.

Intelligent terminals, often in the shape of programmable VDUs do more than merely transmit and receive information. An intelligent terminal has been programmed to make logical decisions about the data that it handles. It can usually vet, edit or validate the data, flag errors in raw input data, etc. Thus, routine processing tasks can be handled without calling upon the main computer.

The capabilities of intelligent terminals vary enormously. Some terminals may incorporate a small cheap mini- or micro-computer, whose sole function is validation. Here, the accepted data may be stored on magnetic tape or disk for a period, prior to being transmitted to the computer centre at a convenient time. This is a helpful yet cheap means of performing various library tasks. The approach combines the flexibility of an online terminal, with lower CPU and telecommunications costs. In an online search of external databases, for example, a microcomputer-based terminal will

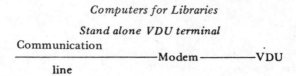

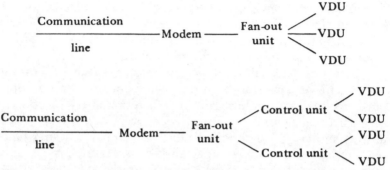

Figure 3.2: Remote VDU terminals

permit the user to develop and record search strategies, before connecting to an external computer, and actually executing the search. The development of the search strategy at the local terminal before connection to the external computer reduces the time spent connected to the external host and thus reduces search and telecommunications costs. For local cataloguing a local microcomputer may store records that are undergoing amendment or creation, whilst they are being processed by the terminal operator, thus removing the need for the terminal to be connected to the main computer until the correct records have been input to the terminal. This again reduces the time used on the main computer to that essential for the new records to be integrated into the larger database. A further possibility is to rely on distributed processing. A local database can be constructed with the aid, say, of a minicomputer and only summary or selected data forwarded to the main computer. This approach has implications for the wide availability of information and centralization.

Telecommunications

In order that computers which are many miles distant from one another be able to communicate with each other, or that a terminal be able to send messages to a computer, it is necessary that there be a medium for the communication of such messages. Communication is usually achieved primarily through a telecommunications network. There are two components of such access: the national and international networks, and the telephone.

There are national and international telecommunications networks which have been designed for transmitting information to and from computers, rather than transmitting people's voices. Most of these networks rely upon a technique known as packet switching. In packet switching the message is split up in order to be sent through the network in short fixed-length packets. Each packet includes the address of the final destination, and the packets travel separately perhaps taking different routes through the network. This means that a large number of messages can be combined together along the same line, giving economies of scale.

Notable telecommunications networks are Tymnet and Telenet, which are predominantly North American, but also have nodes in Europe, and other parts of the world. These two provide access to nearly all major American hosts. Access to Tymnet and Telenet from Europe is possible via agreements with the national Post, Telephone and Telegraph authorities (PTTs). In the United Kingdom the International Packet Switch Stream (IPSS) enables searchers to access computers in North America. IPSS links to Tymnet, Telenet, Uninet and Autonet.

Access to hosts in Europe is facilitated by Euronet Diane. A number of European hosts, including, BLAISE, Infoline, DIMDI and Data-Star are accessible through Euronet. Euronet also provides links to other European networks, such as the Scandinavian network, Scannet. Hosts in Europe can also be contacted through the European part of the IPSS network. Hosts within the United Kingdom may be accessed by a UK user via British Telecom's national network for data access, Packet Switch Stream (PSS). PSS has nodes in many major cities; users pay ordinary call charges to the nearest node, plus a charge for the use of PSS. Provided there is a node within a local call distance, this arrangement is reasonably priced. Normally there is no charge for the use of these networks.

Other hosts also have their own networks. Dialog provides Dialnet as a link between California and London. SDC has a line from the USA to its computer in Woking. ESA-IRS has Esanet which has a node in London. Most computer bureaux which host the factual databases have their own worldwide networks. These private networks are generally cheaper than public networks.

To get into these national and international networks which are suitable for long-distance communication, a telephone link must be used to access the closest node. It is possible to use dial-up access via the public switched telephone network. A leased line connection is useful for heavy users, since it offers higher speeds of transmission, and permits the use of local storage devices. The terminal must be linked to the telephone line via an acoustic coupler or a modem.

A modem is permanently wired, and converts digital messages which the terminal and computer understand into analogue messages capable of being transmitted down telephone lines. Acoustic couplers serve a similar purpose except that they are not permanently wired; the handset is placed in the acoustic coupler to achieve a connection once a telephone line has been opened.

A Local Area Network (LAN) is a relatively new type of network which is used to link terminals and computer systems within one building, or one local area. Because the locations to be served are geographically close high speeds of data transmission are possible. LANs offer interesting possibilities for the future for libraries with scattered (but not too scattered!) service points, and these are beginning to be exploited.

Word Processors

Word processors merit a brief mention because being designed for inputting, editing, formatting, storing and sometimes searching and/or sorting of text and finally its output, they do offer some text-retrieval facilities. A word processor comprises the parts shown in Figure 3.3. Word-processing software is also available, as mentioned previously, for most mainframes, micros and minis. The difference between, say a micro and a word processor is that the word processor is a dedicated machine which cannot be programmed to support other functions. Since the word processor is dedicated it tends to have many of the necessary features of a 'super-typewriter',

Printer — usually high quality
with daisy-wheel or golf-ball
|
Keyboard — ——— Microprocessor ——————— Screen
Alphanumeric +
function keys to |
support editing   Storage, ie
internal RAM
+ backing store, eg disks

Figure 3.3: A word-processing system

such as a high quality printer and a carefully designed keyboard. Word processors cost around £5,000 in a stand-alone
mode, and upwards of that for larger networks. In time it
is likely that general computer systems will take over the
functions of special-purpose word processors.

Micros, Minis and Mainframes

There are three main categories of computer: mainframe
computers, minicomputers, and microcomputers. It is difficult
to define the boundaries between these categories of systems
at all rigidly, but it still remains important to recognize the
different types of application areas of the three different
categories of machine. Figure 3.4 provides a summary comparison of the main features.

A mainframe computer is the most powerful of the three
categories of machine. Such machines are usually fast, have
an extensive range of storage facilities, can support a large
number of terminals, and often offer various special features.
Software packages operating on mainframe can support very
large databases, often with many users, such as those of the
online hosts, and offer the most sophisticated range of
retrieval facilities. Examples of mainframes include the
IBM 370 series, the CDC 7600 series, the ICL 2900 series and
the Honeywell 6000 series. Usually a mainframe will be
acquired by an organization such as a university, local authority, company or research establishment in order to support a
variety of applications across its full range of activities. For
many information units the use of a mainframe involves
sharing facilities. These facilities may be those of the parent
company, or those of a computer bureau. A computer bureau

Feature	Mainframe	Mini	Micro
Physical size	Large	Small, eg 3m by 4m would contain a large configuration	Smaller still, eg typewriter size upwards
Computing power	Depends upon the nature of the application, but generally mainframes are the most powerful, followed by minis and then micros		
Peripherals	Larger range	Smaller, slower and less sophisticated, but quite good	Cheaper and still less sophisticated, but still often adequate
Software	A wide range of utility and applications software, depending on machine	Also a good range of utility and applications software	A good range of certain types of software, but tends not to be as sophisticated as on larger machines
Operating	Needs some full-time, trained and experienced operators	Simpler, but extent of supervision required depends on size of installation	No problems, although librarian is likely to need basic familiarity with maintenance of system, etc.
Environment	Special suites with air conditioning; false floors to cover cables	Ordinary office, etc with some screening to reduce noise from peripherals etc and simple air conditioning with large installations	Ordinary home or office

Maintenance	Contracts, with weekly checks	Contracts with monthly or less frequent checks because less use and less equipment	Contracts usually with call-out checks
Availability	Manufacturer only	Manufacturer, system packages (for types of application), system houses (systems for particular users)	Same outlets as minis, but also retailers and business equipment agents
Price	£100,000 to £2m +	£2,500 to £50,000 +	£50 +

Figure 3.4: A comparison of the main features of mainframe, micro- and minicomputers

sells computer time and support services, and the use of a bureau is a means of accessing sophisticated retrieval facilities in circumstances where it is not otherwise possible to acquire or make use of the hardware that is necessary to support a large database using a full range of text-retrieval facilities.

For most information managers the use of a shared mainframe has advantages and disadvantages. On the plus side shared hardware means that there is expertise and advice on the software package and its implementation available from those running the hardware, and, secondly, hardware is someone else's responsibility (if it breaks down, etc). The disadvantage stems from the necessity of negotiation with whoever does control the hardware. This may be fruitful, but may abound in difficulties.

Mainframes cost between £50,000 and several million pounds.

Minicomputers were first introduced in the 1950s based on integrated circuits. These are generally smaller and correspondingly cheaper than mainframes. Some of the main machines are the PDP11, DEC10 and the VAX series, all from Digital Equipment Corporation. Others include the HP3000 from Hewlett Packard, Data General machines, and the Prime 500 series. Minicomputers are often part of library turnkey systems, and are the size of machine that may be acquired by a library or information unit solely for their own processing. Typically a minicomputer costs tens of thousands of pounds.

Both minicomputers and microcomputers may function in one of a number of modes, amongst which are:

a) Stand-alone system providing independently both batch and online processing;

b) Stand-alone system, linked with other minis to provide a centralized computing resource within an organization, in much the same way as a mainframe;

c) Front-end system where the mini exerts control over the communications between several remote terminals and a mainframe computer;

d) Very intelligent terminal, where the system controls one or more VDU or other terminals;

e) Data-entry system where the data is input, validated, formatted and edited, and then cumulated on some offline medium, or where the mini or micro is linked to some more powerful central resource for further processing.

Microcomputers emerged in the late 1970s when micro-processor-based computers became available. The first micros were based on processors with a word length of 8 bits. Amongst these were the Apple II, Commodore PET, Tandy TRS80 and the Research Machines Ltd 38Oz. More recent micros, such as the Apple LISA and the IBM PC are based on microprocessors with a word length of 16 bits, and 32-bit microcomputers are just entering the market. The more recent 16-bit micros offer increased storage facilities and faster pro-cessing speeds than their 8-bit predecessors. Some of the applications software is still based on the 8-bit micro, but more software is becoming available for the 16-bit micro. Micros at the smaller and cheaper end of the range, eg Sinclair Spectrum, BBC Micro, may be used as home computers, and those at the other end may be used specifically in business, education and industry. These larger machines will support various database-management systems (or perhaps, more strictly, data-management systems) and some will support more sophisticated text-retrieval and library packages.

Further reading

Some Standard Texts on Computers
Note: These texts provide introductory accounts of compu-ters, computing and data processing, and provide useful general background reading.

Atkin, J K *Computer science.* 2nd ed. Macdonald and Evans, 1980.

Fry, T F *Computer-appreciation.* 3rd ed. London, Butter-worths, 1981.

Fry, T F *Data processing.* London, Butterworths, 1983.

National Computing Centre *Introducing data processing.* Manchester, NCC Publications, 1980.

Sheldon, N A *Fundamentals of computing.* London, Hutchin-son, 1984.

Willmott, G *Data processing and computer studies.* London, Edward Arnold, 1982.

Zokorczy, P *Information technology: an introduction.* Lon-don, Pitman, 1982.

Others

Becker, J 'Printer terminals for libraries'. *Library technology reports* 16 (3) May/June 1980. 231-91.

Blair, J C 'Minis, micros and mainframes'. *Online* 6(1) January 1982. 14-26.

Carey, D *How it works: the computer.* 2nd ed. Loughborough, Ladybird Books, 1979.

Fosdick, H *Computer basics for librarians and information scientists.* Arlington (Virginia), Information Resources Press, 1981.

Gilchrist, A (ed) *Minis, micros and terminals for libraries and information units.* London, Heyden, 1981.

Grosch, A N 'The selection of cathode ray terminals for library applications'. *Library technology reports* 18(3) May/June 1982. 273-371.

Hendley, A 'Optical data disks: the archival storage media of the future'. *Communications technology impact* 5(1) April 1983. 3-8.

Rorvig, M E *Microcomputers and libraries: a guide to the technology, products and applications.* White Plains (New York), Knowledge Industry Publications, 1981.

Whitehead, J B 'Developments in word processing systems'. *Program* 17(3) July 1983. 130-53.

Chapter Four

Information structure and software

Any library system must be presented to the computer in terms of the information to be processed, and the instructions on how the information is to be processed. Both the data and the instructions must be coded into a machine-handleable form. The information must also be structured, and the instructions given to the computer in a pattern that the computer understands.

Coding of data
All computerized systems deal with recorded data. To record data, a code must be introduced; even plain written language is merely a code for recording data. Any code system involves the assignment of codes based on symbols from a specified set of symbols occurring at designated positions, to the item being coded. Binary coding is the basis for most representation of data in machinery, because machinery can reliably store and record in two states: '1' and '0'. Computer systems rely upon alphanumeric code systems, and there has been considerable standardization on codes. Some characters represented in two of the more important codes, EBCDIC and ASCII are:

Letter	ASCII	EBCDIC
A	1000001	11000001
B	1000010	11000010
C	1000011	11000011
D	1000100	11000100
E	1000101	11000101

Information structure

A computer handles and stores information in specified formats. The basic component of many computer files is the record. A record is a complete unit of information about a person or item. Each record comprises a number of data items which are organized into locations known as fields. For example, a file of borrower records will contain a record for each borrower, which may have the fields: borrower number, borrower name and borrower address. Fields are determined to suit retrieval requirements. Typical fields in a bibliographic record might be:

   record number
   author(s) name(s)
   title
   publication details
   abstract
   index terms.

These fields will be decided upon in the design of the structure of the record for a particular system and are important when searching, printing or processing the database or parts of it. In larger systems the record format may be determined by the software that has been adopted. However, certainly with many of the DMS and DBMS packages available on micro-computers, it is necessary to set up the record structure. Typically this involves:

a) Creating a data entry form, a screen format which includes all of the necessary fields. It is usually necessary to define whether the information in the field will be alpha-numeric or numeric, and to specify field names and the maximum number of characters in a field.

b) Setting up 'report formats', or in other words, determining the form in which the data are to be displayed when records are selected for various applications.

Fields may sometimes be further subdivided into sub-fields. A title field in a catalogue record might, for example, be divided into title, subtitle and series title.

It is always necessary to label each field (eg author name, pagination), to tell the computer the extent of the field, and to indicate where the field is located within the records. For the author field in a catalogue record, for example, it will be necessary to indicate where the author field starts and where it ends. The nature of this notification depends on whether fixed or variable fields are employed. A fixed field is a field with a pre-determined number of characters. The length of the field and its position in the record is constant for all records, and the computer need only be instructed once for the complete set of records. Such fixed fields are recommended where the number of characters in a piece of information is predictable and stable, eg ISBNs, journal codes, borrower numbers. Variable-length information, such as borrowers' addresses, journal titles and abstracts, compressed into a fixed-field format, will suffer truncation (for long items) or will leave space unoccupied (with shorter items). Nevertheless, some library and information systems use fixed fields with variable-length data and accept the inevitability of truncation.

A variable-field format guarantees compact storage, but needs more complicated program and software routines. The computer can be instructed to note a unique character which designates the beginning and end of each field, eg *,$; or alternatively a directory format can be adopted. Here, a directory accompanies each record, and notes the character position of the start of each field. The directory format facilitates access to individual fields within records and is thus suitable for handling bibliographic files.

Records, then, are comprised of fields. A record may be composed from: a variable number of fields of variable length; a fixed number of fields of variable length; a variable number of fields of fixed length; a fixed number of fields of fixed length.

A file or database is a collection of records in an accessible sequence, stored on an auxiliary storage device such as a magnetic tape or disk pack. Records can be arranged in files in serial or inverted order. A serial file is simply an accumulation of input, with new items added at the end. Retrieval keys, such as indexing terms are stored adjacent to the records to which they relate. Any search must process the complete file, from start to end, seeking matches between terms, ie a sequential search. Serial storage is an inherent limitation of magnetic tape. Serial files are cost effective where the nature of the job means that the complete file must be checked and the file is not too large. Typical applications might be for: selecting current awareness notifications and matching these with users' profiles; or printing a list of overdues in a file of books on loan arranged in accession-number order; or merging into the file, in one pass, the records of books borrowed in a day.

Random-access files must be used for online access. Disks and drums permit random access. The three dimensions of such devices form the basis of three distinct file organization techniques. The first dimension is the extent of a track, the second, the vertical dimension of the cylinder and the third, the range of cylinders or packs.

In serial or sequential mode, records are written in order at successive addresses. Although storage is filled to capacity, this method has the same limitations as when it is used with magnetic tape, ie sequential searching of the whole file is necessary. The direct-access mode involves the use of a key-address transformation computation: a direct relationship is computed between the value of the key and the appropriate address in a range of disk locations. The file is compiled by taking records in turn, computing the disk address, and writing the record into this location. Provision is made for two records which have the same address, although substantial overflow can cause problems. The advantage of the direct-access mode is that access to a record via its primary key is immediate.

In the indexed sequential-access mode, records are first sorted into ascending key order and then written serially on to disk. As each track is filled, the highest key number on the track is written onto a track index; new records are written into the overflow area and, as multiple cylinders are filled, a second-level index is created on a further cylinder. This stores, for each cylinder in the file, the number of the highest key on that cylinder. Similarly, if the file occupies more than one disk unit, a master disk index is created. Thus a hierarchy of indexes (sequential indexes) is created, and access to information is normally via this hierarchy.

In a serial file, each record carries its index terms and other details; but in a direct-access file, the records with common index terms or search keys are linked and thus form an inverted file. An inverted file is similar in concept to a manual index and is normally organized in the indexed sequential-access mode.

Direct-access file organization is impractical and uneconomic due to the disparate frequency distributions of the indexing words; some occur frequently, others rarely. In each case a dictionary is used. In direct access, if numeric codes are provided with the database, the dictionary is needed if profile terms are entered in word form; in text searching, it is needed both during file inversion and query processing. The size of the dictionary can be very large and attempts to restrict its size may lead to the truncation of words. Thus, all random-access files include both the records themselves and an index of keys that direct to records on the file. The index often contains all possible items in the record suitable for use as search access-points.

A file of records is often referred to as a database. A data-base system is a system which integrates a series of separate databases. Chapter five describes the contents and formats of library and information databases more extensively.

Software
All computers need instructing in the manipulation of the data received. These instructions, known as programs or soft-ware, will, for instance, specify how information should be re-arranged for machine storage and how to sort and format the information to suit output specifications. All programs are written in special programming languages.

The most fundamental of programming languages is ma-chine code. Machine code is a binary coding of instructions in the same format as these instructions will be held in the computer, ie a program in machine code is merely an organized sequence of '0's and '1's. Machine codes are unique to a specific computer model and depend upon its internal circuitry; thus, to program in machine code, a programmer must be intimate with the workings of a specific computer. Machine code is potentially the quickest and cheapest programming language in terms of its utilization of machine time, but programs must be re-written for implementation on a different machine and more instructions are likely to appear in the program than with a more sophisticated programming language.

Assembly-code languages represent a slightly more sophis-ticated model than machine code. An assembly-code language uses mnemonic literal sequences to designate the machine codes and to reference storage locations. Programs in assem-bly-code language are translated into machine code by a language program known as an assembler. Some assembly-code languages have become well known (eg PLAN for the ICL 1900 range, BAL for the IBM 360 and 370 series, and USER-CODE for the ICL System 4 series), but they remain specific to a group of machines. Assembly languages are powerful and make for easier program formulation than machine codes. Assembly languages are often used for those parts of a set of programs which will be executed frequently; but assembly language programs are fairly long and prone to mistakes.

Most programs are written in 'high-level' languages, which are more concise and less dependent upon a specific computer configuration. High-level languages are designed to suit the problem area in which they are used. They are thus 'topic specific'.

A program in a high-level language must be translated into machine code before it can be executed. There are two types of programs which may be enlisted to perform this translation: compilers and interpreters. A compiler checks the program statements to minimise the presence of ambiguous or unrecognized statements. A compiler will translate the entire program into machine code before the program is run. Compilers are available for most of the major languages, to run on most of the major types of machines. It is possible to have more than one compiler to support the operation of a programming language on one machine. Different compilers may be designed for efficiency in executing various different tasks. An interpreter operates in a similar way to a compiler, except that instead of producing a program in machine code before execution, it checks, translates and executes each instruction, one at a time. Many microcomputers have interpreters rather than compilers, but using an intepreter is usually slower than using a compiler.

Nevertheless, most programs are written in a few key languages and may thus be run on many computer installations. FORTRAN and ALGOL are the best known science and technology oriented languages; BASIC is a simple programming language, designed to be assimilated in a few hours; and COBOL is a language designed for business data-processing. PL/1 combines the algebraic features of ALGOL with the business data-processing features of COBOL. PL/1 has been relatively popular in library and information systems. Some programming languages, such as BASIC, are available in a number of different versions.

In choosing a language, the availability of the following should be considered: store, support, programming time, processing time. Portability between computer systems, and maintenance or ongoing development of programs should also be taken into account. There are four distinct categories of software: computer operating systems, user-written programs, utility programs and applications packages.

The computer operating system or OS is a set of master programs which supervise the passage of all other programs, and control input and output to peripherals and the compilation of programs. If, for instance, the computer is to be connected via a telephone line to another computer, the OS will have to encompass software to organize this link. The most advanced OSs are multiprogramming systems which debug, compile and execute several programs in parallel. The user of the system can communicate with the OS through a set of OS commands. With mainframes and minicomputers the machines are usually supplied with OSs, and the OS will be different for each family of machines. With microcomputers the most used OS on 8-bit microprocessor machines is CP/M. The 16-bit microprocessors have led to other OSs, such as CP/M-86 and the OS for the IBM PC known as PC-DOS, and UNIX. A related kind of OS, the teleprocessing system, is specifically concerned with controlling peripherals, especially in multiprocessing systems. The quality of the OS determines the processing potential of the system.

Utility programs are written either by the computer manufacturer and/or software houses. Manufacturers will normally supply, as part of their standard support, programs for file creation, sorting and merging and editing of output records. Such routines are common to many applications and library and information systems are no exception.

For more specialized routines, a library system designer may write his own programs, or commission a software house to formulate them. Thus user programs are generated. Many programming tasks are facilitated by the use of subroutines. Subroutines are groups of commands for treating certain situations; they can be utilized in programming as a ready-made unit.

Many tasks on the computer are sufficiently similar for 'packages' of programs to be used. File or database management packages, for instance, provide the capability for executing a variety of basic operations on a file of any format. They usually: establish files and define file formats; maintain files (eg add, change, delete records); search files (to retrieve records or files); prepare reports and other forms of data on files including sorting data, arranging output formats, etc.

Library and information oriented packages have been produced and marketed by computer manufacturers, software houses, academic and research institutions, national bodies and other libraries. A good program package, like an off-the-peg garment, is cheaper, more readily available and possibly easier to implement than a tailor-made system. It is ready immediately and can be expected to be reliable. Documentation should be full, with a detailed system specification, hardware requirements noted, input and output defined and file specifications and systems timing given. Packages can be modified but some of their inherent advantages — costs, timeliness and reliability — will suffer.

Computer manufacturers provide packages for use with their equipment which are cheap, but only available when there is a large audience. Software houses and other organizations concerned to recover the costs of the development of the package offer more tailored but more expensive packages. The next section considers breifly some types of software packages.

Types of packages

1 Basic software or utility software, is made available by computer equipment manufacturers or software houses in order that certain basic functions may be performed; these functions are common to many applications. This software, known as utilities, usually supports basic operations such as data entry and validation, sorting and merging files, and editing data. Different sets of utilities will support different forms or ranges of options for the above operations. For example, simple editing packages are likely to contain commands to insert, delete, print and replace specific lines of text. More sophisticated editors may offer full screen-editing facilities, and automatic input and output.

2 Word-processing and other general-purpose business software: Word-processing packages are available for use on mainframes, minis and micros. These packages are directed primarily towards applications where it is convenient to be able to store a text, and, then later recall this text, modify it, and re-use it. Typical applications are standard letters, reports undergoing editing, forms, compilation of lists, and the updating of manuals. By their very nature word-processing packages must support the manipulation of text, including, for example, alignment of margins, deletion and insertion of sentences, lines, words and paragraphs, back-up files, underline, and arrange for the text to be appropriately placed on the page. Some word-processing software also boasts the ability to merge files, arrange records in a file according to some order (such as alphabetically by name), and search for specific strings within small files.

There are also a number of general-purpose business packages to cover, for example electronic mail, and the maintenance of mailing lists. Other business packages support financial and accounting applications.

3 Database management systems (DBMS) offer some of the facilities which will support text retrieval. Although the nature of DBMS is difficult to define, in general they can be expected to:

 a)   allow applications programs to be written independently of the DBMS control program, and support their being written in a high-level language;

 b)   create and maintain a database, through the exploitation of utility programs;

 c)   allow data to be reorganized to accommodate growth, shrinkage, etc;

 d)   provide data security and access safeguards;

 e)   cope with system failure and generate re-start procedures.

DBMS then, are essentially programming frameworks, although some such systems have been used extensively for text retrieval. The effectiveness of a DBMS for information retrieval depends to a large extent on the ease with which non-programmers can interact with it. Some have query language auxiliary systems which make them less forbidding to a non-programmer. DBMSs handle essentially tabular data or fixed-length fields well, where searching usually involves looking for a specified character in a particular field. These constraints are not a problem where the records comprise largely fixed-length fields and searching can be conducted on pre-assigned keywords. Some larger DBMSs have been used to support significant cataloguing applications, and may also be used for lists for periodical circulation, contact and referral lists, purchase control, etc.

With microcomputer systems most packages are strictly DMS, data management systems, rather than DBMS. DMS software on a micro typically permits retrieval from a file for a single application. In order to achieve this it will include modules for input, editing, storing, selecting, simple processing and output of a file of records.

4 *Free text packages* (FTX) are designed specifically for text retrieval. Typically, the records are independent, of variable length and composed mostly of natural language texts. Primary access is through an inverted file of text terms which are drawn from the records as they are placed on the database. Access is by content, rather than structural position, although most systems provide some option for holding fixed-format data. A particular feature of such software packages is the user-related interfaces. More discussion of such packages, together with some examples, is included in chapter seven.

5 *Expert systems:* An expert system is a complex program based on the rules and knowledge of a specific field of expertise, such as oil exploration, or medical diagnosis. The program is essentially a problem-solving framework, and should contain two principal elements:

a) the detailed rules of the subject area, from which inferences can be made by mathematical logic;

b) the detailed knowledge from which these rules are derived, and which they therefore support.

Using the set of established rules in a diagnostic fashion, the system will process new information in conjunction with the relationships between items of information already stored, to derive conclusions.

For example, in a system for medical diagnosis, the new information may be medical symptoms, and the rules are those by which a doctor would arrive at a diagnosis, and the stored knowledge is information on the symptoms that co-occur in particular diseases. The ES will ask for the symptoms of a patient to be entered, and will search the store for analogous cases. Some such systems are used in conjunction with bibliographic references.

6 *Software associated with external hosts:* Obviously each of the major online hosts have their own software which supports their activities as a host. From experience gained by supporting large databases with many searchers, various of the online hosts have begun to offer 'private file' facilities. With the aid of such facilities users can exploit the extremely sophisticated software of a large host. If the user is already familiar with the command language, etc of that host, then a private file avoids the need for familiarization with a further software package. However, private file facilities can be expensive, since, if the host computer is used, a telecommunication charge will be incurred every time that the file is consulted.

The second category of software generated in association with online searching of external databases supports the more economic access to these hosts. There are various software packages, mainly for use on micros, which support online interaction with an external database and permit, for example, the storage of search profiles locally, and the development and editing of search profiles and search outputs locally.

7 *Library housekeeping software:* In many applications, text-retrieval software may be used alongside or instead of other software aimed primarily at library housekeeping. Most text-retrieval packages will support the creation of files that may be used in library housekeeping and would, for instance, permit catalogues to be created and maintained. Some, however, also offer special cataloguing support facilities, such as the possibility of creating catalogue records in MARC and MARC-compatible formats. There are a variety of packages which are specifically designed to support library housekeeping rather than text retrieval. Some of these are integrated packages covering many functions, whereas others concentrate on specific functions. Housekeeping packages may support some or all of the following: cataloguing, acquisitions and ordering, serials control, circulation control, and in addition management information of various kinds may be offered. More details are given in chapter five.

Information on packages can be obtained from Aslib's file on software, manufacturers, software houses, published literature, courses, exhibitions and colleagues who have already tested the package, as well as some of the sources referred to in chapter one.

Further reading
Note: A number of texts listed at the end of chapter three contain useful basic accounts of relevance to the topics covered in this chapter.

Ashford, J H 'Software cost: making it or buying it'. *Program* 10(4) January 1976. 1-6.

Burton, P F 'Microcomputer applications and the use of database management software'. *Program* 16(3) July 1982. 180-90.

Garoogian, R 'Pre-written software: identification, evaluation and selection'. *Software review* 1(1) February 1982. 1-34.

Grosch, A N *Minicomputers in libraries 1981-2: the era of distributed systems.* White Plains (New York), Knowledge Industry Publications, 1982.

Tedd, L A 'Software for microcomputers in libraries and information units'. *Electronic library* 1(1) January 1983. 31-48.

Uhiaker, T and others 'Design principles for a comprehensive library system'. *Journal of library automation* 14(2) June 1981. 78-89.

Chapter Five

Databases

Databases have already been defined in chapter four: to re-iterate, a database is a collection of similar records, with relationships between the records. This chapter will introduce some of the databases of concern to libraries and information units.

Libraries and information units have always compiled databases. Catalogues, files, lists of borrowers and indexes are all, in a sense, types of databases; they comprise a series of related and similarly formatted records. Although the chapter will dwell mainly on commercially available databases, the same types and formats are suited to locally created databases. The librarian is likely to encounter commercially available databases in various contexts. He may purchase or lease the machine-readable version of the database and process it locally to provide his own services. Alternatively, he may wish to purchase one of the wide range of products that other tape processors are generating from the database. In both circumstances the librarian needs to know a little about the database, since the nature of the database determines the quality and nature of the products that are derived from it.

External databases of central concern to librarians can, for expository purposes, be divided into three major categories: bibliographic databases, non-bibliographic databases and catalogue-record databases.

Bibliographic databases
Bibliographic databases are a major category of database of interest to librarians. (Although catalogue-record databases

strictly also fit into this category, they have been excluded from this section so that they may be treated more fully in the section entitled 'Machine-Readable Cataloguing (MARC) databases'. Bibliographic databases are a series of linked bibliographic records, with each record containing some combination or permutation of the following components:

a) document number
b) title
c) author
d) source reference
e) abstract
f) full text
g) indexing words or phrases
h) citation, or number of references
i) organization originating the document, or author's address, or both
j) language of full document
k) local information, eg location, special classification numbers.

These components then constitute a document reference, which, if used in appropriate databases, may contribute to bibliographic control by facilitating the retrieval of relevant documents when they are needed. Note that such a document reference does not normally give the information itself, but rather indicates documents in which information might be found. Sometimes, an informative abstract does yield valuable direct information even in an essentially bibliographic database.

One such record will be held for each document represented in the database. Some of these components are more commonly used as primary retrieval keys, eg author, title words, journal title; others may be helpful as secondary retrieval keys (ie to limit a search on, say, subject) eg language, local information; and the remaining elements are merely displayed or printed to aid the user in locating, or judging the relevance of, a document.

Bibliographic databases may be created by local information units and other organizations. In addition, there are large, internationally accessible databases which can be searched with the aid of international telecommunications networks.

The above elements are reminiscent of the contents and format of the printed abstracting or indexing bulletin or journal from which the database stems. Most machine-readable bibliographic databases owe their inception to an abstracting or indexing journal, which still remains a primary income source. Some databases and their printed equivalents are:

Database	Printed Equivalent
MEDLARS	*Index medicus*
INSPEC	*Science abstracts*
CHEMABS	*Chemical abstracts*
SCISEARCH	*Science citation index*
Sociological Abstracts	*Sociological abstracts*
ERIC	*Resources in education*
COMPENDEX	*Engineering index*
Psychological Abstracts	*Psychological abstracts*

The result of databases being tied to a printed product may be that the database is not entirely suited to the machine-searching environment. Its coverage may be too universal or too specialized. Access points are likely to be unsophisticated and information update rather slow. The pricing structures also tend to be influenced by the presence of a printed product.

Bibliographic databases can be divided into the following five loosely defined categories:

a) large discipline-oriented databases corresponding to a major abstracting journal such as BIOSIS PREVIEWS *(Biological abstracts)*, CHEMABS, INSPEC, ISMEC (Information Service in Mechanical Engineering).

b) interdisciplinary databases with coverage normally based on key or core journals, eg SCISEARCH and SOCIAL SCISEARCH.

c) cross disciplinary databases, eg METADEX (produced by the American Society for Metals).

d) smaller, more specialized databases serving a particular technology, including those generated by research associations (eg RAPRA Abstracts, from the Rubber and Plastics Research Association), research and data-analysis centres (eg Pollution Abstracts from Data Courier Inc, World Textile Abstracts from the Shirley Institute).

e) databases covering specific types of publication, such as CLAIMS/CHEM (from IFI/Plenum Data Co for US chemical patents), Comprehensive Dissertation Abstracts (from Xerox University Microfilms), and NEXIS (from Mead Data

Central, covering various newspapers).

Many databases are not the product of one organization, but are the outcome of a co-operative endeavour. For example, INIS (International Nuclear Information System) is run under the auspices of the International Atomic Energy Authority in Vienna. The scanning, abstracting and indexing is conducted by agents in twenty-one or so countries. The Technical Information Center of the US Energy Research and Development Administration provides coverage of United States literature for INIS. One output is INIS *Atomindex,* a printed indexing journal. Likewise, in another co-operative venture, the British Library covers British medical literature for the US National Library of Medicine in exchange for access to the MEDLARS database. A similar agreement is in force between the American Chemical Society, the Chemical Society and Gesellschaft Deutscher Chemiker for national input and marketing.

Again, in selecting databases, it is important to recognize that there are overlaps in coverage between databases. A large scale study of *Engineering index, Chemical abstracts* and *Biological abstracts,* confirmed suspicions of overlap and coverage. Further, in-house databases are often derived partly or entirely from more comprehensive databases. Several references in the further readings list give lists of databases.

One of the chief merits of a machine-readable database is the potential for marketing a variety of information services by formatting one set of input. Each service is tailored to meet a distinct need. Typical database products include:

Selective Dissemination of Information (SDI)
Group SDI
Standard SDI
Online SDI
Printed abstracting and indexing journals and their indexes
Batch retrospective searching
Online retrospective searching
Magnetic tape services (ie buy or lease tapes)
Review services (ie current awareness listings of reviews in a relatively wide subject area)
Thesauri
Classification schemes
Lists of journals covered (ie a list of journals in a subject)
Reports (of tests, evaluations and practice)

Computer software
Some of the more significant of these products are treated at
more length in chapters seven and eight.

Institute for Scientific Information Products and Services
Arts and humanities citation index
ASCA topics
Automatic new structure alert (ANSA)
Automatic subject citation alert (ASCA)
Chemical substructure index
Current abstracts of chemistry and index chemicus
Current bibliographic directory of the arts and sciences
Current chemical reactions
Current contents
Current controversy
Index chemicus registry of organic compounds
Index to scientific reviews
Index to scientific and technical proceedings
Index to social sciences and humanities proceedings
ISI atlas of science
ISI/BIOMED
ISI/Compumath
ISI/Geo scitech
ISI/Index to scientific and technical proceedings and books
    (ISI/ISTP&B)
ISI machine-readable data bases
ISI press
ISI search service
Journal citation reports
Original article text service (OATS)
Request-a-point
Science citation index
Science citation index, abridged edition
Sci-mate
Scisearch
Social sciences citation index
Social scisearch

**Figure 5.1: Some products from a related group of databases from one
producer**

Non-bibliographic databases

The librarian's preoccupation with bibliographic databases is understandable, but not shared by the world at large. The majority of machine-readable databases comprise series of records which although formatted in a similar fashion to bibliographic databases store actual information rather than references. Sometimes referred to as databanks, these databases provide answers, facts and data. Those non-bibliographic databases that the librarian or information officer is most likely to encounter are those that are accessible via the same channels as bibliographic databases, that are publicly available, and which store the directory-type data to which a library has traditionally provided access. Such databases cover business and economics, social sciences and education, and science and technology.

Librarians will also encounter non-bibliographic databases in library housekeeping systems. For example, there is little bibliographic about a file of borrowers' names and addresses. Such a file gives information directly. Such files will be considered more fully in the appropriate chapters.

The business and economics databases include economics and financial statistics, industry-specific statistics and corporate financial information. For example, Dialog alone provides access to around a dozen numeric databases in the fields of business and economics. These include:

BI/DATA FORECASTS
BI/DATA TIME SERIES
BLS CONSUMER PRICE INDEX
BLS EMPLOYMENT, HOURS AND EARNINGS
BLS LABOR FORCE
BLS PRODUCER PRICE INDEX
DISCLOSURE II
PTS INTERNATIONAL FORECASTS
PTS US FORECASTS
PTS US TIME SERIES
US EXPORTS

Amongst these, the PTS databases originate with Predicasts Inc. PTS INTERNATIONAL FORECASTS, for instance, contains summaries of published forecasts with historical data for all countries of the world (except the United States). Coverage includes general economics, all industries, detailed products, and end-use data. Information is extracted from a wide range of international sources, including statistical reports of industries and trade associations, newspapers, and publications of the UN, and other international organizations. Another database from Predicasts, PTS US TIME SERIES is composed of two subfiles. *Predicasts Composites* contains about 500 time series on the US, giving historical data and projected consensus of published forecasts through to 1990. Coverage includes population, GNP, per capita income, employment, production, etc. The other subfile, *Predicasts Basebook,* contains annual data from 1957 for about 37,000 series on US production, consumption, prices, foreign trade, etc. A database from a different producer, Business International Corporation, BI/DATA TIME SERIES, consists of up to 317 economic indicators represented in time series records for up to 131 countries. Coverage is primarily economic and marketing-related activities such as production and consumption statistics, balance of payments, etc.

Still in the area of business and economics there are an increasing number of directories and other sources available in full-text form online. Many reference sources that were previously only available in hard copy can now be consulted on paper, on microfilm or online. Some examples are:

1) *ICC database:* a directory of every limited company in Great Britain, from which can be extracted data on individual companies, indicators of average performance for sectors of industry, and cross database searches in accordance with user's own criteria. The database is available online direct, via Dialog or on viewdata;

2) *Dun and Bradstreet — Dun's Market Identifiers 10+* presents detailed information on more than one million US business establishments. Included are current address, product, financial and marketing information for each company;

3) *D & B Principal International Business* presents information on the leading companies in 133 countries. Names, addresses, annual sales, number of employees, type of company, are amongst the information provided for each company;

4) *EIS Industrial Plants* includes information on around 90% of total US industrial activity. It is produced by Economic Information Systems Inc;

5) *Harvard business review/Online* provides the complete text of all articles from 1976 to the present, published in the *Review*. References to earlier articles are also included. The records contain the bibliographic citation, an abstract, the complete text, cited references, titles of any graphs or exhibits that may appear in the article, and thorough indexing.

6) *LEXIS* and *NEXIS* are important databases from Mead Data Central. In addition to LEXIS's coverage of reported cases since 1945, there are twenty-nine series of law reports including:

All-England Law Reports
Building Law Reports
Criminal Appeal Reports
Local Government Reports
Patent Cases
Weekly Law Reports

NEXIS covers various financial, business and economic newspapers, such as *American banker, Bond buyer, Washington post,* and various magazines, including *ABA banking journal, Bank administration, Business week, Chemical engineering, Dun's business month,* and the *Oil and gas journal.* Since 1983, NEXIS has covered material previously available through the New York Times Information Bank.

7) *EUROLEX* offers access to law reports and other legal sources. Many of the databases are full text. Four series are available:

Law of Jurisdictions within the United Kingdom
Laws of the European Communities and other European jurisdictions
Industrial and Intellectual Property Law
Taxation Law

In addition to business and economics databases there are a number of non-bibliographic databases or databanks with chemical, and other scientific information. As with the business and economics databases, some of these are only available online, whilst others are online full-text versions of directories and encyclopaedias which were previously available in printed form. Two examples of directories which have recently become available in online format are the third edition of the *Kirk Othmer Encyclopaedia of chemical technology* and *Martindale Online. Kirk Othmer Online* may be searched through BRS, and is published by John Wiley & Son. *Martindale Online* originates with the Pharmaceutical Society of Great Britain and can be searched on their own computer. Services such as CAS-Online and Télésystèmes DARC offer the possibility of searching chemical structures online.

An increasing number of general directories are also becoming available online. Some such are:

American men and women of science
Biography master index
Encyclopaedia of associations
Marquis Who's who
Ulrich's International periodicals directory

Various services are available which could broadly be described as dealing with current affairs. Finsbury Data Services' Textline, for example offers current facts, figures and comments from a wide range of business publications. The BBC's World Reporter Service contains the full texts of news stories prepared for transmission.

This can only be a very brief overview of some of the increasing number of non-bibliographic databases. There are many omissions and examples only are given. An estimate provided by the European Association of Information Services indicated that there are around 1,500 databases and databanks available, or potentially available, for public searching in western Europe.

Machine-Readable Cataloguing (MARC) databases

MARC databases are a rather specialized type of bibliographic database in that their use in the library tends to be largely in the context of housekeeping routines rather than in information retrieval. In this context libraries often select from the external MARC database, and compile their own database to coincide with their stock.

The acronym MARC is applicable to any machine-readable cataloguing record but tends to be applied in a rather special context. MARC refers to the databases of catalogue records generated by the Library of Congress (USA) and the British Library Bibliographic Services Division for the *British national bibliography* (BNB). Catalogue records not included in these databases may be termed *Extra-MARC* Material or EMMA.

The main centralized MARC databases include:

1) *LC MARC*, 1968 to date, covering books of all subjects including fiction, and updated monthly. The records are produced by the Library of Congress.

2) *UK MARC*, 1950 to date, covering British books and first issues of serials titles on all subjects including fiction, and updated weekly. The records are produced by the British Library Bibliographic Services Division.

3) *A VMARC*, 1960 to date, covering non-book materials, with particular emphasis on audio-visual materials used for teaching purposes, and covering all subject areas.

Several national bibliographic agencies are engaged in the production and distribution of machine-readable records. Those that are now well established include countries such as Canada, Australia, West Germany and France. It is hoped that an international MARC network will soon be established, but this awaits progress in technology, cataloguing standardization and the speed of production of catalogue records. Several bilateral arrangements already exist.

The MARC record format
The MARC record format was designed by the Library of Congress and the British Library with the object of being able to communicate a bibliographic description in machine-readable form in such a way that records could be re-formatted for any conceivable purpose. Early trials around 1966, conducted by the Library of Congress, worked with the MARC I format; but this format was jettisoned in 1967 and superseded by MARC II or MARC, as it is usually called.

As more countries have exploited MARC, variations in practices have spawned deviations from the original format. The UNIMARC format is a new format for international exchange of MARC records. National organizations creating MARC records use national standards within the country and re-format records to UNIMARC for international exchange. Hence, the MARC record structure is not identical worldwide, but the UK MARC format suffices as an illustration of the record format. UK MARC and UNIMARC comply with ISO 2709, the standard for bibliographic interchange on magnetic tape.

The MARC format includes up to sixty-one data elements of which twenty-five are directly searchable. The format is compatible with the second edition of the *Anglo-American cataloguing rules* (AACR2) and the nineteenth edition of the *Dewey Decimal classification* (Dewey 19) and can be expected to be modified in order to accommodate any new editions of these tools.

The MARC format comprises two sections: section 1, which gives information describing the bibliographic data and section 2, which holds the bibliographic data itself. Thus the segment of magnetic tape relating to an individual record could be imagined as:

Record Label	Directory	Control Fields	Variable Data Fields

The fields that comprise section 2, and thus hold the bibliographic data, are all variable length fields; and hence, it is necessary to signal the beginning and end of each field. So, each field is preceded by a three-character tag and two numeric indicators, and ends with a special delimiter. Tags consist of three numerals within the range 000-945. The tags have a mnemonic structure in that they follow the order of a catalogue record, and the tags for added entries mirror those for main headings. For example, the chief tags are:

100 Personal author main entry heading
110 Corporate name main entry heading
240 Uniform title
245 Title and statement of responsibility
250 Edition and statement of edition author, editor, etc
260 Imprint
300 Collation
400 Series statement
500 Notes

Now, also, a personal author's name generally has '00' in the second and third positions, so that:

100 is used for a main entry personal author heading;
600 is used for a personal author subject heading;
700 is used for a personal author added entry heading.

Each of the main fields also has two field indicators; these are single-digit numerals which follow the tag, and are unique to the field to which they are assigned. Indicators are used to distinguish between different types of information entered in the same field, to provide for title added entries, to indicate

```
001          001       [0851572987]      General  Monograph  Format      (Sept.81)

Leader       LEA       Status[3]       Type[a]        Analyt[ ]        Source[B]

008          008       Date on File [801117]    Pub Date [s1980    ]   Country [uk]
                       Illus[     ]  Int Lev[ ]   Phys Med[ ]  Form Pub[     ] Govt[0]
                       Conf[0]       Lit Text[ ]    Bios[ ]      Lang [eng]
015 0 00  *aB8007202+
017 0 00  *a0210/0+
021 0 00  *a0896644367*bv+
040 0     *bMP+
050 0 00  *aZ678.9+
082 0 10  *a022*b.9+
083 0 00  *aLibraries. Applications of digital computer systems+
100 0 10  *aRowley*hJ E+
245 0 10  *aComputers for libraries*d(by) J.E. Rowley+
260 0 00  *aLondon*bBingley*c1980+
300 0 00  *a159p*c23cm+
350 0 00  *a$4.50 : CIP rev.+
440 0 00  *aOutlines of modern librarianship+
504 0 00  *aBibl. - Index+
650 0 00  *aLibraries*xAutomation+
690 0 00  *z11030*alibraries*zs0030*aapplications*vof*win*z31030*adigital
              computer systems+
692 0 00  *a0007668+
692 0 00  *a0000035+
981 0 00  *aROWLCOMP1980+
982 0 00  *aCOMFOLI 1980*dOUTOFMOL1980+

General record from UNION      Local record from UNION
LIBCODES   SH   MP   GR   PP   NL   PN   PR   SU   BN   TP   SK   WP   OX   CA   BE   RT   CR
           WS   LP   DL   AU   BR   BU   BI   WK
UNRELEASED RECORDS
CMD ?


001          001       [0851572987]      Local  Monograph  Format      (Sept.81]

Leader       LEA       Status[1]       Title A/E[ ]     CA Excl[ ]      Sp Coll[ ]
                       Retro [ ]     No Of Copies[02]

008          008       WIP [ ]   Loan[ ]       Wants[ ]     Sp Class[ ]    How Obt[ ]
                       Dept Sugg [    ]   Phys Form[ ]    Bind Code[ ]    Sp Coll[ ]
                       UC Code  [   ]     Bib Int[ ]     Stat Anal[ ]

009 A    *a352158+
009 B    *a352157+
030 A    *aC+
030 B    *aC+
060 0    *a022.9+
065 0    *aROW+
200 A    *a4HL18+
200 B    *a4HL18+

General record from UNION      Local record from UNION
UNRELEASED RECORDS
CMD ?
```

Figure 5.2: A record from BLCMP showing the MARC record format

the number of characters to be dropped in filing titles and to show whether information, such as edition and imprint, relate to a part or the whole of a multi-part work. For instance, in the field for main entry corporate author heading, the following indicators are used in conjunction with the 110 tag:

Inverted corporate heading	110.00
Government heading	110.10
Direct order corporate heading	110.20

Many fields in a catalogue record contain smaller distinct units, known as subfields. Typical subfields in the imprint area are place of publication, publisher and data of publication. All subfields are preceded by a subfield code, which consists of a single symbol (cg '£') and a single letter. The imprint might be coded as: 260.00 £a London £b Weidenfeld and Nicolson £c 1979.

Subfield codes are defined in the context of the field in which they are used, but similar codes are used in parallel situations. For example, the subfield codes for a person's name are constant, regardless of whether he is main, or additional author or subject.

Having completed the variable data fields we can return to section 1. The control fields are only part of section 1 that is input by the cataloguer. These contain data such as record control number (eg ISBN), language of the text, intellectual level code, country of publication code, and control access to the main record.

Each record starts with a label and a directory, both of which are supplied by the program. The label contains information about the record, such as, for example, its length and status (new, changed, etc), type and class. The directory is a finding list, which lists, for every tag, the tag, the number of characters in the field, and the starting character position within the record.

The structure of the MARC record is deliberately complicated, to facilitate flexibility. Almost any element can be used as an access point and each element can be of any length.

Bibliographic record formats in non-cataloguing applications

Most of the centralized and shared cataloguing projects take account of and probably use the MARC record format. This degree of standardization is not the pattern outside this specific area of application. Essentially there are two different categories of systems which may be encountered: external databases and local systems suppported by software packages.

For the large databases, there has been little pressure to accept a standard format, and each database producer has in general chosen a record format to suit his particular database. A review of the variety of citation practices which may be encountered in abstracting and indexing services for referring to periodical articles should be sufficient to demonstrate the differences between the elements to be included in a record between different agencies. Let us examine some citations as demonstrated by Figure 5.3, which shows one record in the form in which it appears for the different hosts. Even one database may emerge in different record formats according to the host on which it is mounted.

Yet another variable factor is the growing presence of full-text databases, they will naturally demand a somewhat different record format from bibliographic records if the information is to be appropriately displayed. However, although separate formats have been created for different systems, there are some standards. Various large abstracting and indexing cooperative ventures or networks have developed their own formats. Thus there are groups of organizations with common subject interests who exchange data and cooperate in the creation of international databases. Amongst these can be numbered: INIS (International Nuclear Information System), IRRD (International Road Research Documentation System), CAS (Chemical Abstracts Services), BIOSIS (BioSciences Information) and AGRIS (Agricultural Information System). All of these networks have standard record formats, although it is regrettable that they all operate to different standards.

The record formats to be encountered in local systems which are supported by software packages are many and various. Some of these software packages offer cataloguing systems which will work in a MARC record format, or which produce records which are compatible with the MARC record format. Others do not offer such an option. Virtually all software packages offer the purchaser the opportunity to evolve a record format which suits a specific application. Thus, in local systems there may well be great variability in record format, as designs are implemented within the parameters set by the various software packages.

The *UNISIST Reference manual for machine-readable bibliographic descriptions,* and the record format that it proposes, UNIBID, is an attempt to offer a standard record format for use by abstracting and indexing services, independent of any existing description or cataloguing rules. The first edition of the *Manual* was prepared by the UNISIST/ICSU-SB Working Group on Bibliographic Description, and was published in 1974. In 1976 the UNISIST International Centre for Bibliographic Descriptions (UNIBID) was established by the British Library in collaboration with Unesco, and revision of the *Manual* was undertaken, which led to the publication of the second edition in 1981. Also published, in 1982, was *The Reference manual for machine-readable descriptions of research projects and institutions.* A pilot project is under way to develop and complete portable software to support the application of both manuals. Software already exists to support the record format, specifically Unesco's CDC/ISIS and the International Development Research Centre, Canada's MINISIS, but neither of these packages is portable across many machines, although both are available internationally. This software is important to the further implementation of the record format, especially in developing countries.

Figure 5.3 shows one record coded according to the UNIBID reference record format. It may be profitable further to compare UNIBID with UNIMARC. UNIBID has less redundancy and covers more types of bibliographic material than UNIMARC, whereas the latter probably has more entry points for catalogue headings. While the UNIBID format is used by a number of national and international information systems, UNIMARC, in itself, so far has not been implemented, although plans exist for interchange between MARC-oriented national bibliographic agencies, and it is intended to extend UNIMARC to cover all of the materials covered by ISBDs. Unesco has also started work on the development of the CCF, which is intended to be a universal exchange format suitable for any type of library or information system. Publication, after testing, is imminent. CCF is likely to be compatible with UNIMARC and the UNIBID format.

Evaluation of databases — a checklist
We have insufficient space to consider at any length the selection and evaluation of databases and their products, but

Sample COMPENDEX record on DIALOG

```
1439359    EI8312099359
DISSOLUTION RATES OF URANIUM COMPOUNDS IN SIMULATED LUNG FLUID.
Kalkwarf, Donald R.
   Battelle, Pacific Northwest Lab, Richland, Wash, USA
   Sci  Total Environ  v 28 Jun 1983,  Biol Availability of Trace Met:  Chem
Estim,  Ecol and Health Implic,  Proc of the Hanford Life Sci Symp,    21st,
Richland, Wash, USA, Oct 4-8 1981 p 405-414  CODEN: STENDL
   Languages: ENGLISH
   Maximum  dissolution  rates  of  uranium  into  simulated lung fluid were
measured at 37 $degree$  C to estimate clearance rates from the deep  lung.
The materials tested included: ore and yellowcake,  an airborne sample from
an industrial site,  and certain purified samples.   A batch procedure was
developed  to  test  samples containing as little as 10  $mu$  g of natural
uranium.  Values of dissolution halftimes varied from 0.  01 day to several
thousand  days  depending on the physical and chemical form of the uranium.
Dissolution occurred predominantly by formation of an ion identified in the
paper;   as a result,   tetravalent  uranium  compounds  dissolved  slowly.
Dissolution  rates  of  size-separated yellowcake aerosols were found to be
more closely correlated with specific surface area  than  with  aerodynamic
diameter.  12 refs.
   Descriptors: *BIOLOGICAL MATERIALS-*Chemistry; URANIUM COMPOUNDS-Environ-
mental Impact; AIR POLLUTION; CHEMICAL REACTIONS
   Identifiers: CLEARANCE RATES FROM DEEP LUNG
   Classification Codes: 461; 801; 804
```

No part of this figure may be reproduced or transmitted in any form or by any means, electronic or mechanical, including photocopying or by an information storage and retrieval system, without permission in writing from Engineering Information, Inc., 345 East 47th Street, New York, NY 10017, USA.

Sample COMPENDEX record on BRS

```
AN EI 8312-099359.
AU Kalkwarf-Donald-R.
IN Battelle, Pacific Northwest Lab, Richland, Wash, USA.
TI DISSOLUTION RATES OF URANIUM COMPOUNDS IN SIMULATED LUNG FLUID.
SO Sci Total Environ v 28 Jun 1983, Biol Availability of Trace Met:
   Chem Estim, Ecol and Health Implic, Proc of the Hanford Life Sci
   Symp, 21st, Richland, Wash, USA, Oct 4-8 1981 p 405-414.
MJ BIOLOGICAL-MATERIALS.
MN Chemistry.
ID CLEARANCE-RATES-FROM-DEEP-LUNG.
XR URANIUM-COMPOUNDS: Environmental-Impact.  AIR-POLLUTION.
   CHEMICAL-REACTIONS.
CC A461.  A801.  A804.
CD STENDL.
AB Maximum dissolution rates of uranium into simulated lung fluid were
   measured at 37 degree C to estimate clearance rates from the deep
   lung.  The materials tested included: ore and yellowcake, an
   airborne sample from an industrial site, and certain purified
   samples.  A batch procedure was developed to test samples containing
   as little as 10 mu g of natural uranium.  Values of dissolution
   halftimes varied from 0.01 day to several thousand days depending on
   the physical and chemical form of the uranium.  Dissolution occurred
   predominantly by formation of an ion identified in the paper; as a
   result, tetravalent uranium compounds dissolved slowly.  Dissolution
   rates of size-separated yellowcake aerosols were found to be more
   closely correlated with specific surface area than with aerodynamic
   diameter.  12 refs.
LG EN..
```

Figure 5.3: Sample records on different hosts

Sample COMPENDEX record on DATA-STAR

```
AN  EI 8312-099359.
AU  Kalkwarf-Donald-R.
IN  Battelle, Pacific Northwest Lab, Richland, Wash, USA.
TI  DISSOLUTION RATES OF URANIUM COMPOUNDS IN SIMULATED LUNG FLUID.
SO  Sci Total Environ v 28 Jun 1983, Biol Availability of Trace Met:
    Chem Estim, Ecol and Health Implic, Proc of the Hanford Life Sci
    Symp, 21st, Richland, Wash, USA, Oct 4-8 1981 p 405-414.
MJ  BIOLOGICAL-MATERIALS.
MN  Chemistry.
ID  CLEARANCE-RATES-FROM-DEEP-LUNG.
XR  URANIUM-COMPOUNDS: Environmental-Impact.   AIR-POLLUTION.
    CHEMICAL-REACTIONS.
CC  A461.  A801.  A804.
CD  STENDL.
AB  Maximum dissolution rates of uranium into simulated lung fluid were
    measured at 37 degree C to estimate clearance rates from the deep
    lung.  The materials tested included: ore and yellowcake, an
    airborne sample from an industrial site, and certain purified
    samples.  A batch procedure was developed to test samples containing
    as little as 10 mu g of natural uranium.  Values of dissolution
    halftimes varied from 0.01 day to several thousand days depending on
    the physical and chemical form of the uranium.  Dissolution occurred
    predominantly by formation of an ion identified in the paper; as a
    result, tetravalent uranium compounds dissolved slowly.  Dissolution
    rates of size-separated yellowcake aerosols were found to be more
    closely correlated with specific surface area than with aerodynamic
    diameter.  12 refs.
LG  EN..
```

Sample COMPENDEX record on SDC

```
AN  - 83-099359
TI  - DISSOLUTION RATES OF URANIUM COMPOUNDS IN SIMULATED LUNG FLUID.
AU  - KALKWARF DONALD R
OS  - Battelle, Pacific Northwest Lab, Richland, Wash, USA
SO  - Sci Total Environ  v 28 Jun 1983, Biol Availability of Trace Met: Chem
      Estim, Ecol and Health Implic, Proc of the Hanford Life Sci Symp, 21st,
      Richland, Wash, USA, Oct 4-8 1981 p 405-414 (STENDL)
LA  - ENGLISH
CC  - 461; 801; 804
IT  - *BIOLOGICAL MATERIALS--Chemistry; URANIUM COMPOUNDS--Environmental
      Impact; AIR POLLUTION; CHEMICAL REACTIONS
ST  - CLEARANCE RATES FROM DEEP LUNG
AB  - Maximum dissolution rates of uranium into simulated lung fluid were
      measured at 37 degree C to estimate clearance rates from the deep lung.
      The materials tested included: ore and yellowcake, an airborne sample
      from an industrial site, and certain purified samples.  A batch procedur
      was developed to test samples containing as little as 10  mu g of natura
      uranium.  Values of dissolution halftimes varied from 0. 01 day to
      several thousand days depending on the physical and chemical form of the
      uranium.  Dissolution occurred predominantly by formation of an ion
      identified in the paper;  as a result, tetravalent uranium compounds
      dissolved slowly.  Dissolution rates of size-separated yellowcake
      aerosols were found to be more closely correlated with specific surface
      area than with aerodynamic diameter.  12 refs.
```

Figure 5.3 continued

SERIAL ARTICLE (A/S)

Mavaddat, F. and Parhami, B. (Department of Mathematics
and Computer Science, Arya-Mehr University of Technology,
Tehran, Iran). A data structure for family relations.
Computer Journal, 22(2). May 1979. ISSN 0010-4620, pp. 110-
113.
Abstract:- A data structure is proposed which enables
efficient determination of family relations of common
interest with the minimum amount of information on each
individual.

Implementation codes
Character position 6: Type of bibliographic entity: S
Character position 9: Bibliographic level: A

Data fields

AØ1	ØØ@ØØØ1Ø-462Ø	ISSN
AØ3	Ø5@1ComputerßJournal	Title of serial (Key title)
AØ5	ØØ@222	Volume number
AØ6	ØØ@22	Part number
AØ8	Ø1@1Aßdataßstructureßforßfamilyßrelations	Title of analytic
A11	Ø1@1Mavaddat.ßF.	Author - analytic
A11	Ø1@1Parhami,ßB.	Author - analytic
A14	ØØ@1Arya-MehrßUniversityßofßTechnology+DepartmentßofßMathematicsßandßComputerßScience@2Tehran@3IR	Affiliation - analytic
A2Ø	ØØ@111Ø-113	Pagination - article
A21	ØØ@119790500	Date of publication
*A22	Ø3@119770600	Date received by journal
A23	ØØ@ØENG	Language of document (coded)
*A44	ØØ@1Aßdataßstructureßisßproposedßwhichßenablesßefficientßdeterminationßofßfamilyßrelationsßofßcommonßinterestßwithßtheßminimumßamountßofßinformationßonßeachßindividual	Abstract
A51	ØØ@ØGB	Country of publication code

Figure 5.4: Record according to the UNIBID reference record format

evaluation is important. The following criteria are a useful skeleton for the examination of databases:

a) Coverage: appropriate subject and type of material; comprehensiveness; overlap with other services;

b) Currency and frequency of updates;

c) Easc of use and user subjective preference;

d) Output, eg content of references; abstracting quality; form (card, microform, paper); online or offline; extent of output;

e) Indexing language and variety of access points or searchable fields, in terms of desired retrieval performance;

f) Cost and who is to pay;

g) Documentation, including classification schemes, thesauri, training manuals, etc;

h) Machine compatibility.

This eight-point plan should form a helpful starting base, but obviously needs to be interpreted to meet assorted situations. Some of these situations are explored in subsequent chapters, and the student should attempt to examine how these criteria might be employed in evaluating various databases and their products.

Further reading
British Library. Bibliographic Services Division *UK MARC manual*. 1st standard ed. London, BLBSD, 1975.

Dierickx, H 'The UNISIST reference manuals and UNIBID standardization for development'. *Program* 17(2) 1983. 68-85.

Dierickx, H and Hopkinson, A *Reference manual for machine-readable bibliographic descriptions*. 2nd rev. ed. Paris, Unesco/General Information Programme and UNISIST, 1981. (PG1/81/WS/22).

EUSIDIC database guide, 1983 Oxford, Learned Information, 1983.

Hall, J L and Brown, M J *Online bibliographic databases: a directory and sourcebook*. 3rd ed. London, Aslib, 1983.

Hopkinson, A et al (ed) *UNIMARC Handbook* London, IFLA International Office for UBC, 1983.

IFLA Working Group on Content Designators *UNIMARC: Universal MARC format* London, IFLA Office for UBC, 1977.

UNIMARC: Universal MARC format. 2nd rev. ed. London, IFLA International Office for UBC, 1980.

Chapter Six

Information-retrieval systems and the computer

Information-storage and retrieval systems have become almost synonymous with computers, but manual systems do still exist, and certainly were in evidence before the advent of computers. This chapter and chapters seven to nine discuss facilities for the retrieval and dissemination of information or documents, as distinct from systems which support library housekeeping activities, which are the central concern of chapters ten to thirteen. Nevertheless, although there is a category of computerized systems known as information-retrieval systems, many of the systems which will be considered in the next few chapters are not true information-retrieval systems, in the sense that they do not directly yield the information. Such systems do exist, but their scope is relatively limited, and in order for library and information workers to exploit the full range of information that might be available from a large number of sources, in a wide variety of different formats, many of the systems used in libraries contain bibliographic databases. Such databases provide a basis for document retrieval, and not true information retrieval. There is a growth in the number of full-text databases available through internationally accessible networks, and obviously, many individual organizations design their own databases from which information on matters of interest to that organization can be gleaned. Nevertheless, many of the systems familiar to library and information workers as information-retrieval systems remain only document-retrieval systems. It would require immense storage capacity to retain all of the information currently stored in the vast number of printed documents available in libraries in a computer store.

All information-retrieval systems may be viewed as comprising three stages:

Indexing ⟶ Storage ⟶ Retrieval

In order to discuss the role of the computer in each of these three stages it will be helpful to review these three stages in manual or card-based information-storage and retrieval systems, and to make use of the three stage model as a framework in which various types of systems can be compared.

In such systems, the human indexer assigns index terms to a document or item of information. He selects the topics to be represented by the index terms on the basis of a subjective, but mostly consistent, judgement of the subjects described in the document. He then matches these subjects to index terms, which he believes are likely to be 'sought' by a subsequent searcher. These two, three or more index terms for each document may be drawn from an indexing language, which is controlled (ie there is an accepted list of terms which are to be used in the index) or uncontrolled (ie the indexer uses any terms that he deems suitable). With the index terms selected, a record is made of these assigned terms and an inverted file is compiled (ignoring certain post-coordinate systems), such as a card index or a printed index. This index constitutes the store.   Retrieval is the process of locating documents and items of information that have been committed to store. In retrieval, a searcher describes his subject of interest in concise terms, which he regards as headings likely to be found in an index. If his initial search terms are not present in the index, the searcher can be expected to try alternative terms until his imagination or patience is exhausted. A well-constructed index will prompt and give guidance in the selection of such terms. To what extent has the computer impinged upon this sequence of activities?

Indexing
The assignment of indexing terms in a computerized system may be intellectual, as in a manual system, or machine-assigned. A machine selects index terms according to a set of instructions. Selection must depend on word occurrence and no longer upon the subjective assessment of content, or on the assignment of 'sought terms'. The indexing is no longer geared to a particular item. Lists of indexing terms are

usually established for all items entered. Computers may also be enlisted merely to arrange humanly assigned index terms. The computer acts as a reliable work-horse for arranging index entries alphabetically with respect to one another, for index printing or machine storage of the resultant index. Alternatively, the computer can be programmed to arrange index terms within index entries and also to generate a series of entries or references from one string of index terms.

Storage

Information-storage and retrieval systems may use the computer itself to store the indexing records, or keep the information that the computer has sifted and arranged in paper or microform indexes.

Computer-generated printed indexes are more readily available in a greater variety of formats than their manually produced counterparts. For instance, author, subject, trade-name indexes can easily be generated from one input. In addition, it is easier to issue new editions and cumulate the index.

Computer files may be regarded as the store in which index records are held. File organization has been discussed in chapter four.

Retrieval

The retrieval process is very dependent upon the indexing and storage stages, which to a large extent determine the optimum strategy for searching an information-storage and retrieval system. But another factor which influences the retrieval process remains constant. The system user and the questions that he brings to the system are not, in general, affected by the system. The user's needs do not change merely because he is faced with a computer-based information-retrieval system, even though he may recognize that certain questions are more suited to a computer-based system. Of course, with time and experience, a user may come to expect more from a computer-based system, and as users become more sophisticated systems may need to evolve appropriately.

Machine-produced printed indexes can, in principle, be consulted in the same way as manually-produced printed indexes. But the nature of machine-produced indexes varies greatly, and the searcher will have more success if he recognizes some of their limitations. Some indexes, especially those based on intellectually assigned strings of index terms, are likely to include very specific entries, several access points per item, and plenty of guidance. Others, notably crude machine-assigned indexes, are scandalously devoid of helpful annotation.

Retrieval from a machine-held file may be by direct interrogation of the computer files, or by batch submission of queries. This facility opens information-retrieval avenues that lead into the realms of science fiction. The features of searching in this context introduce a flexibility of search not possible with manual systems and highlight new issues associated with retrieval, such as the economics of information and who should pay, and security and access to files. The computer, then, may offer a much wider range of retrieval possibilities than could be made available without a computer.

The main content of the next few chapters on information retrieval and the computer will be divided into four sections which reflect the main products of computerized information-retrieval systems as they are likely to be encountered in most libraries. One of the features of computerized systems is the possibility of producing a gamut of products, all based on the same input and database (see Figure 6.1).

In some instances, the librarian will himself be responsible for the system and will generate information services; he will regard these as in-house services. Here he generally has considerable control over the system and its end-products. In other circumstances, he will be concerned to evaluate and select from the services offered by external suppliers. In both cases the range of types of services available may be very similar, but the librarian's view of them will differ. Subsequent chapters discuss databases, and some of the products of computer-based information-storage and retrieval systems.

Local databases and systems vs external databases and systems
All types of information database and many of the products derived from them may either be maintained and produced in-house or externally. Libraries and information units are likely to have some contact with both external and in-house databases and their products, and both can be used to complement each other. Libraries with user groups with special interest profiles or with special collections are particularly

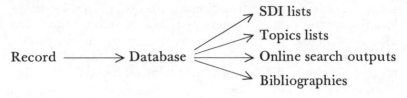

Figure 6.1: Some of the products in which any one record may be used

likely to evolve local databases. Thus, special libraries, such as industrial and government libraries, are most likely to be involved in local databases, whilst public and academic libraries, have traditionally been less involved with maintaining local information-retrieval systems. All types of libraries and information units have however engaged in access to external databases. In general, then, it is worth trying to make some broad comparisons between the two categories of system. What are the differences between retrospective online searching, a printed index, and a current awareness service from an external vendor, and similar products from a local database? Figure 6.2 attempts to make some generalizations which should help to indicate why both categories of system are important, but, like all generalizations, these can probably be found to be inaccurate in some specific instances.

Table 6.2: Local systems vs external systems

Feature	*Local systems*	*External systems*
Coverage	Less extensive of published literature but may include local documents, eg internal research reports, correspondence	Probably cover greater numbers of documents in published literature, yielding wider discipline perspective
Cost	Costs are set-up and maintenance of database costs and, as such, may be quite high, and are more likely to relate to size of database than to extent of use	Costs are incurred per search; occasional searches incur low total costs
Retrieval facilities	Will suit local requirements, in terms of index terms, searchable fields and form of records	May have similar range to local database, but more likely to be a greater range of more sophisticated facilities; user needs more skill in selection
Training for users	Will vary depending on local environment - can be important role for information professionals	Training schemes are well established, but they may be regarded as expensive
Products	Usually a more limited range of products since audience requirements may be less diverse	As full a range of products as can be marketed
Audience	Smaller, more coherent group with less diversity in interests	Larger group - discipline grouped, but employers will be various, eg industry, government, education

Chapter Seven

Retrospective searching

Retrospective searching of databases can be performed by consulting printed abstracting and indexing journals, commissioning a batch-processed machine search, or by conducting an online machine search. In all cases the searcher is desirous of finding most, some, or all that has been published in certain categories over a period of years.

Criteria for machine searching

All searches, retrospective or current awareness, involve the following steps, although it is possibly more important to identify them in this context:

    a)   identification and clear exposition of user's request;

    b)   translation of the request into the language of the system;

    c)   comparison of the codification of the request with descriptions of the documents in the database;

    d)   selection of documents that match the search criteria;

    e)   receipt and browsing of these documents, or information about them, by the searcher.

The first of these steps is common to any searching environment, but needs to be tackled explicitly if an intermediary, and not the end-user, plans to conduct a machine search. Criteria collected at this stage that are frequently applied in order to limit the volume of a search reply include:

subject

author

journal title

use to be made of reference

approximate acceptable size of output

level of treatment of subject, eg introductory or advanced

language

date of publication
country or organization of origin
availability of full text, abstract, translation.
Only with the search fully stated can we proceed to a consideration of how the search will be conducted.

The computer is a valuable ally in retrospective searching, and it is reasonable to suppose that eventually most searches will be performed with the aid of the computer. However, currently, traditional manual searching of printed indexes is satisfactory for queries that can be expressed by a single-subject index heading. Quests for basic unchanging statistics and background information are still quite adequately, and often more comfortably, answered by monographs, directories, dictionaries and encyclopedias in print form.

Searches for which the computer represents considerable economy of effort or money fit into one or more of the following categories:

1 Searches where abstracting and indexing journals or bibliographies, and some where directories, might otherwise be searched.

2 Searches where flexibility is important, and it is useful to be able to change or modify search strategy in the light of knowledge acquired during the search process (iterative searching).

3 Searches where it is not possible to search in a printed index because either: a) the terms that best express the topic are not present in the index; or b) for precision the search must be expressed as a complex logical statement linking a series of index terms.

4 Searches where the timed period covered by the machine-readable database is adequate. In general this period is less than 15 years.

5 Searches where an extensive bibliography is the expected output. Machine searching and printing bypasses much clerical slog.

6 Searches where machine searching is deemed the most economic alternative. This factor is rather difficult to evaluate since the cost of the search (currently about £1 per minute, or £10 to £20 per search) is not the only consideration. Other important factors are the manner of costing staff time and the willingness to pay of the end-user. Many libraries, particularly public and academic, have never charged for information

services, but the high unit cost of machine searches is causing them to reconsider this stance. Such machinations may have far-reaching repercussions on the philosophy of public and academic library services.

7   Searches where machine searching of databases outside the library's normal printed stock of indexes is helpful. Special libraries find it especially useful to be able to perform occasional searches in areas outside their own speciality.

There are also environments in which the computer search is accepted as being more attractive or impressive than an equivalent and perfectly satisfactory manual search. If a user is prepared to pay for and/or conduct a machine search in preference to a manual search because he enjoys the experience, then who is the librarian to deny him? If the librarian or information officer does not tap the public's imagination, then someone else, often less well versed in information retrieval, will.

The above list of suitable searches not only discriminates between machine and manual searches, but also goes some way towards explaining the popularity of online searching, to the detriment of batch searching. In the sixties, the majority of computer-based searches were batch processed, but this is no longer the case.

A batch search commences with the completion of a form, not unlike that which is used as a basis for SDI profiling. This form is then dispatched to an agency or centre for profile construction, as in SDI, save that the profiles must be more selective than SDI profiles, and hence, often more sophisticated. When the profile has been framed and coded, it is run, together with other searches, in a batch and usually in off-peak time, against a computer-held file. Document records matching the search request are printed and sent, usually by post, to the requester.

Batch searches will continue to be used in some in-house installations where the volume of requests is low; but even in this environment, mini- and microcomputers have reduced its impact. Generally, as many of the early tests on MEDLARS confirmed, batch searching is unsatisfactory.

Batch searching is slow (long turn-round time) and permits no modifications to the profile. Even after waiting a week, the search output may be slight, irrelevant, too voluminous, or unsatisfactory in some other unforeseen manner. Where batch processing retains its hold it is accompanied by online profile compilation, or is used to print, offline, references selected during online searching. The remainder of this chapter is devoted to online retrospective searching. The other option for retrospective searching, printed indexes, is considered more fully in chapter nine.

International systems offering online search facilities

Search systems with online access may be under the control of a local information unit or an external vendor. In both cases, searching is via an online terminal that is, a teletypewriter or VDU terminal connected via a telecommunications network to a computer or series of computers. Within a compact site the terminal can be hard-wired to the computer. Otherwise, for remote terminals, the telephone network is generally used via either leased or dial-up lines. Diagrammatically this may be summarized as:

Terminal ⟷ Telecommunications network ⟷ Computer

Telecommunications networks have been discussed in chapter three. These sections concentrate on the agencies which maintain computers with databases which can be searched internationally.

There are a number of major suppliers of online search services who mount databases on a computer and sell access to these databases. These organizations are known as online service suppliers, online spinners, or online hosts. The larger online hosts offer access to a number of databases — sometimes these hosts are referred to as supermarket hosts. Amongst the supermarket hosts might be numbered Dialog, SDC ORBIT and BRS. Other hosts offer access to a more limited number of databases. These hosts are likely to be the producers of the databases to which they provide access. Amongst such hosts are the organizations responsible for mounting Martindale (Pharmaceutical Society of Great Britain) and LEXIS and NEXIS (Mead Data Central). STN International is a programme being mounted by Chemical Abstracts Services whereby software and other expertise is shared amongst potential and actual hosts in such a way that it is more possible for individual database producers to act as hosts for their own databases. Thus database producers may mount their own database and make it accessible through international telecommunications networks, rather than leasing the database to one of the supermarket hosts. As more database producers explore this possibility there may be a proliferation of hosts. The next few pages introduce briefly, some of the major hosts.

SDC ORBIT

The Systems Development Corporation's (SDC) search service runs ORBIT from a computer in Santa Monica, California. ORBIT has been operational since 1972 and has around seventy databases mounted. ORBIT is the exclusive vendor for around half of its databases. Many of the SDC files are scientific and technical. Several of the exclusive databases cover petroleum and fossil fuels. These include APILIT from the American Petroleum Institute which covers magazines, journals, papers and reports. APIPAT, also from API, covers refining patents from various countries. TULSA is the equivalent of the printed *Petroleum Abstracts.* Other databases include several offering access to US government information such as CRECORD, the index of the Congressional record, and FEDREG, the *Federal Register.* Also available are other assorted databases, including ACCOUNTANTS (index), SPORT (printed equivalent is *Sport and Recreation Index),* and WPI *(World Patents Index,* covering the patent specifications issued by patent offices in major industrial nations).

SDC ORBIT also offers certain special services. These include an SDI service and the facilities for users to establish and maintain their own private databases. *Electronic Maildrop* is an online document-ordering feature, where documents can be ordered from various suppliers. The *Data Base Index* is an online database of basic index terms used in any of the SDC databases and helps users to determine which files are most likely to supply information on a given subject. Training programmes, search aids and various publications all support the SDC ORBIT services.

Dialog

Dialog information retrieval services is run by Lockheed Information Systems (LIS) from a computer in Palo Alto in California. Over one hundred databases are available, of which around half could be broadly categorized as scientific and technical. Large scientific and technical files include CA SEARCH, SCISEARCH and BIOSIS PREVIEWS. However, the scope of the databases is wide, and extends to the arts, social sciences, public affairs, current events and business. Included are ART MODERN (printed equivalent *Art Bibliographies Modern*), AMERICA: HISTORY AND LIFE, and MANAGEMENT CONTENTS. Most of the databases are bibliographic in nature, but Dialog does offer some statistical and dictionary files. Amongst these are the ENCYCLOPEDIA OF ASSOCIATIONS, EIS INDUSTRIAL PLANTS and Predicasts INTERNATIONAL TIME SERIES and FORECASTS (see also p58 above).

SDI is available on a number of databases. DIALORDER is an online ordering service; document requests are supplied by one of twenty-two suppliers. The Dialog Private File Service allows organizations online access to the private files, and permits subscribers to build and maintain their own files. Various search aids and training facilities are offered.

BRS

Bibliographic Retrieval Services Inc (BRS) is run from Scotia, New York. A relative newcomer to the marketplace, having commenced operation in 1977, BRS is a small host offering access to around thirty databases. Its policy is to acquire databases that are heavily used, and although no attempt has been made to acquire exclusive rights to databases, nine of its databases are not available from any other source. These nine are either in medicine or serials. BRS offers MEDLINE, and also, ALCOHOL USE/ABUSE, DRUG INFO and other medical databases not available through other supermarket hosts. BRS also has two serials files. These are the National Agricultural Library's NAL SERIALS, and MARC SERIALS which lists serials catalogued by the Library of Congress. Another interesting database, is BOOKS-INFO, a file of bibliographic data on books in print, from Brodart Inc. Other databases are ERIC, MANAGEMENT CONTENTS, SOCIAL SCISEARCH, CA SEARCH and INSPEC. Some large files are only online for the most recent three- to five-year portions.

BRS offers an SDI service. Also available is a cross database for multi-file searching (BRS/CROSS), online accounting, private database services and an online catalogue service. Prices tend to be lower than those on SDC and DIALOG, and this has obvious attractions. The range of databases has attracted a number of academic libraries.

ESA-IRS
The European Space Agency's (ESA) Information Retrieval Service (IRS) was first established in the form of the European Space Research Organization's Space Documentation Service. (ESRO SDS) in 1965. Based at Frascati in Italy ESA-IRS was one of the first organizations to offer online search facilities. Databases originally focussed upon space research and technology. Now ESA-IRS offers access to thirty-five databases, mostly in science and technology. ESA-IRS has back-up services in various European countries; the service offering such facilities in the United Kingdom is IRS-DIALTECH.

INFOLINE
Pergamon-INFOLINE came into being in its present form in 1980 when it was taken over by Pergamon. Based in London, Pergamon-INFOLINE offers around twenty to thirty databases of various types and sizes. Databases include: CA SEARCH and COMPENDEX, both large scientific databases. Smaller bibliographic databases include: WORLD TEXTILES, ZINC, LEAD & CADMIUM ABSTRACTS, RAPRA ABSTRACTS. Directory databases include: DUN & BRADSTREET'S KEY BRITISH ENTERPRISES, FINE CHEMICALS DIRECTORY, and the DIRECTORY OF COMPANIES.

BLAISE
The information-retrieval services offered by BLAISE are split into two components: BLAISE-LINE and BLAISE-LINK. BLAISE-LINE offers access to a number of bibliographic files which are held on a computer in the United Kingdom. A search of these files may be useful for compiling bibliographies, identifying information, verifying references, and in the ordering of photocopies and loans. Access is available from any suitable terminal to BLAISE subscribers. BLAISE-LINK provides access to files in the biomedical and toxicological areas, which are available on the computer of the National Library of Medicine (US). These databases include MEDLINE, which gives references in all aspects of medicine, psychology, physiology, pharmacology, veterinary science, dentistry and nursing. The CANCERLINE files cover cancer, TOXLINE and RTECS cover toxicity and pollution information respectively, POPLINE covers references on fertility, contraception and demography, and

HEALTH is for non-clinical aspects of health care. For the librarian, CATLINE, SERLINE and the NAME AUTHORITY FILE give authoritative records of books and serials held by the National Library of Medicine. Various supporting services are available for the BLAISE-LINE file. AUTOSDI is a current awareness service. Document ordering is available through the Automatic Document Request Service, which provides a link to the British Library Lending Division. OFFSEARCH is a means of running a search, overnight, on more than one database, in a cost-effective mode. The BLAISE-LINE and BLAISE-LINK Search Services are available to those who do not have access to a terminal and wish BLAISE to conduct the occasional search on their behalf. Training manuals and support services, such as the Help Desk, are a particular feature of the BLAISE information-retrieval services.

DATA-STAR
DATA-STAR, offered by Radio-Suisse, mounts various databases including: business databases, eg ABI/INFORM, PREDICASTS, MANAGEMENT CONTENTS, FINANCIAL TIMES COMPANY INFORMATION; biomedical databases, eg BIOSIS PREVIEWS, MEDLINE, EXCERPTA MEDICA; chemical databases, eg CHEMICAL ABSTRACTS, and CHEMICAL ENGINEERING ABSTRACTS; and technical databases, eg NTIS, INSPEC and COMPENDEX. Altogether between twenty and thirty databases are offered.

BELINDIS
BELINDIS, the Belgian Information and Dissemination Service is offered by the Data Processing Centre of the Belgian Ministry of Economic Affairs. Around ten databases are offered, with notable databases being EAI (Economics Abstracts International), CREDOC-BLEX (Belgian legislation) and INIS (International Nuclear Information System). These reflect the general coverage which is particularly in the areas of law and legislation, economics and energy.

ECHO
ECHO is the European Commission's own host service. Since 1980 it has offered access to databases and databanks either wholly or partially sponsored by the Commission of the European Communities. Databases are mainly of a European

nature, including information on research organizations and a multilingual terminology databank to user guidance files.

Other European hosts include DIMDI, the German Service, and Télésystèmes-Questel based in France. Both of these hosts offer around thirty-five databases each. There are now over twenty online hosts connected to Euronet, offering altogether access to around 150 databases. All of the major European hosts mentioned above are linked into Euronet.

Hosts for non-bibliographical databases

Non-bibliographical databases include numeric textual-numeric, properties and full-text databases. Non-bibliographic databases are offered by many more suppliers than bibliographical databases, and are particularly used for businesses and industry to extract information in the fields of business, economics, trade and commerce. Such hosts are more likely to be accessed by end-users, such as economists and managers, than information workers. Frequently numeric databases and the hosts which support them permit some computation and manipulation of the retrieved data.

The most significant suppliers of non-bibliographical databases are:

1   *Automatic Data Processing Inc* (ADP), which offer a number of financial and economic databases with the aid of their new TSAM (Time Series Analysis and Modelling) on the DATALYST service. Included are the UK-Macro-CSO (Central Statistical Office), and the International Financial Statistics Databases.

2   *IP Sharp,* which makes available a number of public databases including the UK CSO, the International Monetary Fund and the US Consumer and Wholesale Price Indexes, via the MAGIC software which allows for the manipulation of time series and non-time series data.

3   GEISCO is a US service offering information on mineral resources in the USA, and over 95 other countries. Included are the BI/DATA databases which contain almost 20,000 time series covering the economics of one hundred different countries. MAP (Management Analysis and Projection System) is available for manipulating the data.

4   *Business International Inc.* is another US service covering economic and marketing activities in over seventy countries.

5   *Data Resources Inc,* again US-based, covers databases in economics, finance, energy and weather.

6   *SIA* in the United Kingdom covers information in travel and transport, economics in EEC countries, construction of nuclear power stations, and financial information.

Viewdata and Teletext

Viewdata systems were conceived as a means of providing easy access to information held on a central computer. Access is via a modified television set, a telephone (and its connections) and a simple keypad. Prestel is British Telecom's viewdata service, and was started in 1979. Although the original aim of British Telecom was to penetrate the domestic market, most of the terminals are in the business sector. Many public libraries participated in various of the Prestel trials. The information available on Prestel changes as the information-providers come and go. The information is provided by around three hundred information-providers which gives around 160,000 screens of information that can be viewed. Information-providers pay a fee to British Telecom, and may then charge users for each frame that they consult. Access to frames is through a menu-based system, whereby the user is offered a number of options on each screen and must choose the appropriate label for the information that he wishes to retrieve by keying the appropriate number. Viewdata services are being made available in other countries, including Canada, Finland, France, the Netherlands, Switzerland and West Germany. Closed user groups, for organizations such as the travel trade have been popular, and some large organizations are establishing their own viewdata systems.

Teletext services are broadcast information services which may be accessed in a non-interactive mode. These services may be accessed with a television and a telephone line, but tend to be limited in the quantity of information that they can carry, and so may be mainly restricted to summary financial and business statistics, news (international, national and local) and weather, etc. Such services offer a useful publicly available information service.

Hosts: points for comparison

Database hosts must be compared and contrasted in order that a sound selection of host may be made for any specific search. Obviously, the overall objective is to retrieve as many relevant, and as few irrelevant, documents in the minimum time and at the least cost and user inconvenience. Although hosts offer similar services, and the pressures of the marketplace mean that any vital facility must be offered by all of the major hosts, there are differences between the services offered by the different hosts. Apart from the different databases available, there may be differences in the way in which any given database can be searched under various hosts. For some databases the selection of the database will determine the host, but on other occasions other factors must also be considered. Specifically then, hosts may vary in respect of:

1   *The databases offered:* As already explored the numbers of databases offered by any specific host will vary, as can the subject coverage and language of the available databases. Also, different hosts may have different time-spans of any given database available for online searching.

2   *Search facilities:* The elements of records that can be searched may differ from one host to another. Certainly the field formats may vary and the field names may be different. Some systems offer more extensive facilities with regard to contextual or proximity searching, and truncation. For non-bibliographic databases various special facilities may be required.

3   *Command languages* are an essential feature of the search facilities of any given host. Figure 7.1 summarizes and compares some differences between hosts. A command language is the language with which the search proceeds; the commands are the instructions that the searcher can issue to the computer. Different hosts have different command languages depending upon their search software.

4   *Formats for records:* Various formats are available for viewing the details of retrieved references. Sometimes it is possible for the searcher to select the elements that he requires, but in searching other hosts only a few standard formats are available.

| COMMAND | [HOST] | | |
FUNCTION	DIALOG	SDC	ESA/IRS
Prompt	?	USER:	?
Change files	.FILE BEGIN	FILE	.FILE BEGIN
Execute a search	SELECT SELECT STEPS COMBINE	(FIND)	SELECT COMBINE
Precedence of Boolean operators	1. NOT 2. AND 3. OR	1. AND 2. NOT 3. OR	1. NOT 2. AND 3. OR
Look at inverted index	EXPAND	NEIGHBOR	EXPAND
Specify level of postings detail	————	AUDIT	————
Restrict search	LIMIT	(date ranging)	LIMIT
Save information for later use	END/SAVE	STORE	END/SAVE KEEP
Remove saved items from storage	.RECALL (name) .RELEASE	PURGE (name)	.RECALL (name) .RELEASE
Look at answers online	TYPE	PRINT	TYPE
Print answers offline	PRINT	PRINT OFFLINE	PRINT
Cancel offline print order	PR—(set no.)	(Done within PRINT command)	PR—(set no.)
Order original document	ORDERITEM	ORDER	ORDER
View session history	DISPLAY SETS	HISTORY	DISPLAY SETS
Restart session	BEGIN	RESTART	BEGIN
Send message to vendor	————	COMMENT	MESSAGE
End the online session	LOGOFF	STOP	LOGOFF

Figure 7.1: A simple comparison of some commands for different online hosts

5 *Additional facilities:* Many hosts offer other facilities in addition to the basic online search facility. Often SDI or document delivery services are available. These may become increasingly important as hosts seek to match the needs of users more closely.

6 *Support services:* Most hosts offer some support and training services. Help desks, training courses, manuals, newsletters and other search aids can influence the effectiveness of a searcher. Good training and careful instruction can often lead to a searcher being effective with even the most complex searching systems and databases. The availability of such support services must be considered, but availability is not the only factor. Support services must be effective, accessible (eg training courses in the searcher's own locality), and reasonably cheap.

7 *Time availability:* Most hosts are not available twenty-four hours a day, seven days of the week. Some down-time is necessary for maintenance and updating of the files. Hosts are available for a variable number of hours in the day, and a variable number of days in the week. For example, DATA-STAR is available on Mondays from 10.00 to 18.30, and on Tuesdays to Fridays from 8.00 to 18.30 (Central European Time). Times should be sought which coincide with the user's requirements.

8 *Cost:* The cost of searching a specific database for a given search can be difficult to assess, but is obviously an important aspect of the searching process. There will be special rates for additional services such as SDI or document delivery. Normally, charges will comprise database connect charges, and print charges per reference. Telecommunications charges will also add to the cost of a search. The database connect charges sometimes include database royalty charges, but for other hosts these will be charged separately. Print charges are usually charged per reference retrieved, with online and offline prints often attracting different tariffs, and different record formats being charged at different rates. But matters are not as straightforward as merely analysing the direct costs. If extensive use is likely to be made of a particular database discount charges are available by contracting to buy a predetermined number of connect hours per year.

9 *Experience:* The searcher's experience with a specific host may be an important factor in determining his search effectiveness. Thus, from the searcher's point-of-view it is important not only to assess the specific features of the host, but also to examine his own skills.

The online search

The detailed analysis of the features of an effective online search are explored more fully in other texts, such as Hoover, Houghton and Convey, and Meadow and Cochrane. Here, the intention is merely to demonstrate the elements of a retrospective online search, so that each of these elements may be considered at greater length in another context. An online retrospective search will be performed at an online terminal. The first stages must involve the clarification of the request, which results in a clear specification of the information required, and, secondly, the choice of the database in order to perform a search which is likely to be successful. After these preliminary planning stages have been negotiated the user logs on to the system which has been chosen according to the criteria listed in the previous section, and normally any news about the system will be first displayed. Following successful logging-on, the user will be invited to select a database. Once a database has been selected the search proceeds as the user introduces a series of commands and search parameters, and the computer responds to instructions. The search involves making use of four elements: search or index terms, logic, commands, and various other facilities. Each of these are demonstrated in the example in Figure 7.1 but in order to clarify their use each is briefly introduced below.

1 Search or index terms

The search or index terms are the terms used to describe subjects in the retrieval process. Depending upon the system and the database, a variety of fields may be searched for index terms. Sometimes there are special fields in which subject-type index terms are stored, and in some databases much of the search specification makes use of these terms. In other databases, with other hosts, it may be possible to search on the text in all fields of the record, such as the author field, the text of the abstract, the full text of the document, and various elements of the bibliographic citation such as the

A Typical Dialog Search

Shown below is a suggestion of the kind of a conversation you might have with DIALOG during a typical search. On the facing page is a replica of the actual printout that would be generated at your computer terminal during the search.

From start to finish the search took less than five minutes. During that time more than 20,000 documents were examined and eighty pertinent ones were identified.

PURPOSE OF THE SEARCH: You want to find the sources of recent articles on *the effect of stress on executives.*

WHICH DATABASE TO SEARCH? DIALINDEX, the online subject index, shows you that File 15 ABI/INFORM contains information about articles on business and management.

Here, in effect, is what takes place at your computer terminal.

What you say to Dialog	How Dialog responds
1 I'd like to search File 15, please.	What would you like me to find for you?
2 Do you have any articles that include the word *stress* or the word *tension?*	Yes, I have 1564 that refer to *stress* and 395 that include a reference to *tension* for a total of 1840 documents that mention either or both terms.
3 How many articles do you have that mention *executives* or *managers* or *administrators?*	I have the following references: *executives*—7072; *managers*—14,435; *administrators*—997; for a total of 20,707.
4 How many of those articles or documents contain the terms *stress* or *tension* AND ALSO the terms *executives* or *managers* or *administrators?*	460.
5 I'm interested only in *recent* articles. How many of those 460 were published during 1981?	80.
6 I'd like the following information about the first of those 80 documents: record number, title, journal title, date, pages, and an abstract on the article if available.	Title of the article is "Executive Stress: Pressure in a Grey Flannel Suit." It's by Roger H. Lourie and appeared in Direct Marketing Magazine, volume 44, number 8 on pages 46 to 49 of the December 1981 issue. An abstract of the article follows: (For complete text of the abstract please refer to the sample printout on the facing page.)
7 For the next 9 articles please give me only the basic information, no abstracts.	(For detailed response, see printout at right.)
8 Thank you, I'm finished. Please log me out and give me a record of this search and its cost.	This search was made on February 19, 1982 and completed at 11:54:10 A.M. The user's identification number is 3468. Cost for computer time was $5.91. Time required to conduct the search was 0.081 hours. The search was made in File 15. Six descriptive terms were used to make the search. Communications cost (TELENET) was $.49 and the total estimated cost was $6.40.

If you had wished to do so you could have requested that the references be printed offline and mailed to you, typically more cost effective if many references are desired.

Most databases contain abstracts or summaries of the original document such as that shown in our sample search. Often these abstracts provide enough information to answer your question. Should you decide that you want to order the full text of the article abstracted, you can do this easily while still connected to the DIALOG computer through Dial-Order, DIALOG's online ordering system. You simply type .ORDER and just the record number from the upper left of each reference.

This search is an example of how simple yet powerful a DIALOG search can be. As you grow in familiarity with DIALOG you'll find yourself taking advantage of the many additional search capabilities that can improve the speed, increase precision, or lower costs.

Figure 7.2

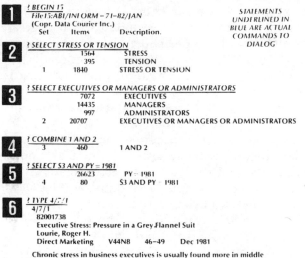

1 ? *BEGIN 15*
File15:ABI/INFORM – 71–82/JAN
(Copr. Data Courier Inc.)
Set   Items   Description.

*STATEMENTS
UNDERLINED IN
BLUE ARE ACTUAL
COMMANDS TO
DIALOG*

2 ? *SELECT STRESS OR TENSION*
       1564   STRESS
        395   TENSION
1   1840   STRESS OR TENSION

3 ? *SELECT EXECUTIVES OR MANAGERS OR ADMINISTRATORS*
       7072   EXECUTIVES
    14435   MANAGERS
        997   ADMINISTRATORS
2   20707   EXECUTIVES OR MANAGERS OR ADMINISTRATORS

4 ? *COMBINE 1 AND 2*
3   460   1 AND 2

5 ? *SELECT S3 AND PY = 1981*
    26623   PY = 1981
4   80   S3 AND PY = 1981

6 ? *TYPE 4/7/1*
4/7/1
82001738
Executive Stress: Pressure in a Grey Flannel Suit
Lourie, Roger H.
Direct Marketing   V44N8   46–49   Dec 1981

Chronic stress in business executives is usually found more in middle management than in top management. It is characterized by a continuous sense of time urgency and an incessant need to accomplish too much. Such changes in work pattern as concentrating on only the important items, taking frequent "day dreaming" breaks, and staying an extra half hour to avoid rush hour traffic can help relieve stress. Transcendental meditation, biofeedback, encounter groups, and yoga are also useful in understanding and relieving tensions and stress. However, more important than any artificial technique is an individual's self-realization that he is exhibiting outward symptoms of stress and inner tension and that he must personally take action to reduce this pressure-building situation. The current emphasis on stress-relieving techniques helps make the public aware of the dangers of stress.

7 ? *TYPE 4/3/2-10*
4/3/2
82001706
Preventing Environmental Stress in the Open Office
Rader, Martha; Gilsdorf, Jeanette
Jrnl of Systems Mgmt   v32n12   25–27   Dec 1981

4/3/3
82000967
Managing Stress for Increased Productivity
Huber, Vandra L.
Supervisory Mgmt   v26n12   2–12   Dec 1981

4/3/10
81027568
Does Your Head Hurt?
Cohen, Irving I.
Inc.   v3n12   117,119   Dec 1981

8 ? *LOGOFF*
19feb82 11:54:10 User3468
$5.91   0.081 Hrs File15 6 Descriptors
$0.49   Telenet
$6.40   Estimated Total Cost

Figure 7.2 continued

date or journal title. Normally it is possible to specify the field in which a search term is to be found for a match.

The terms on which searching is based may be controlled or natural language. Controlled indexing language are sets of terms which have been deemed to be suitable for indexing a particular subject area, a particular collection, or a particular type of document or information. Such indexing languages are normally recorded in thesauri or lists of subject headings. Most of the larger bibliographic databases have a thesaurus or list of subject headings from which terms are drawn and allocated to records. Thus, there is the INSPEC thesaurus, for example, which lists the terms to be found as index terms on the records in the INSPEC databases. Similarly SHE, Subject Headings for Engineering, is to accompany the COMPENDEX database. In most databases with most systems it is usually possible to conduct searching on the text in the record (in addition to index terms), and in this situation searching is performed on the natural or uncontrolled language of the record.

2 Command languages

A command language is the set of commands or instructions that the searcher uses to instruct the computer to perform certain operations. Negus has identified fourteen basic functions for which commands must be present in any online command language. This set of commands forms the basis for the Euronet Common Command Language, which is available for searching on some of the European hosts. These same functions are also seen to be important in framing the International Standard for Command Languages.

These command functions are:

CONNECT	to provide for logging on
BASE	to identify the database to be searched
FIND	to input a search term
DISPLAY	to display a list of alphabetically linked terms
RELATE	to display logically related terms
SHOW	to print references online
PRINT	to print references offline
FORMAT	to specify the format to be displayed
DELETE	to delete search terms or print requests

SAVE   to save a search formulation for later use
                    on the same or another database on the
                    same system
OWN   to use a system's own command when
                    the general system, in this case Euronet,
                    does not cater for a specialized function
                    available on a particular system
STOP   to end the session and log off
MORE   to request the system to display more
                    information, for instance to continue the
                    alphabetical display of terms
HELP   to obtain guidance online when in diffic-
                    ulty

As can be seen in Figure 7.1 which compares the commands
for several hosts there is no standard command language. The
different command languages are associated with the different retrieval software used by the different hosts. As far as
users are concerned, standardization of command languages is
highly desirable. The need to become familiar with different
command languages for different hosts is a considerable
barrier to effective retrieval. In particular, when one command
means one thing in one system and something else in another
system this is likely to lead to confusion. Hosts are less keen
to standardize, although the Euronet Common Command
Language has been adopted by various hosts, and there is
some recognition of the potential benefits to the user of
greater standardization.

3 Logic

Embedded in the search commands there is normally the
potential for introducing search statements which make use
of a search logic. There are basically two types of search
logic, Boolean, and weighted-term search logic. The former is
the most prevalent. Search logic is the means of specifying
combinations of terms which must be matched in retrieval.
The terms linked by the search logic into a search statement
may be drawn from free or controlled index languages.
Profiles usually need to be more complex with free-language
searching as greater provision for the entry of documents
under synonyms and related terms is necessary. In an online
search the search statements are evolved one at a time, and

feedback is available at each stage. Figure 7.2 demonstrates this process.

Figure 7.3 demonstrates and introduces the Boolean operators, OR, AND and NOT, and begins to demonstrate how they may be used in search statements. Figure 7.2 takes this one step further by demonstrating how these search statements are incorporated into a complete online search.

The other search logic, weighted-term search logic is less common, although there is a growing interest in its potential. In most search statements it is possible to designate certain concepts as being more significant than their neighbours. In its role in formulating search profiles, weighted-term logic may be introduced either as a search logic in its own right, or as a means of reducing the search output from a search whose basic logic is Boolean.

In an application where weighted-term logic is the primary search logic, search profiles are framed by listing search terms and assigning each term a weight. This weight reflects the significance of the term to the subject being sought, and thus places a relevance rating on a document which is found containing that term as a search term. Search profiles combine terms and their weights in a simple sum, and items rated as suitable for retrieval must have weights which exceed a specified threshold weight. A simple SDI type profile showing the use of weighted-term logic is shown below:

Search Description The use of radioactive isotopes in measuring the productivity of soil.

A simple search profile (which does not explore all possible synonyms), might be:

8	Soil	4	Plants
7	Radioisotopes	3	Food
7	Isotopes	2	Environment
6	Radioactive	2	Agriculture
5	Radiation	1	Productivity
5	Agricultural chemistry	1	Water

A threshold weight appropriate to the specificity of the searchers' enquiry must be established. For instance a threshold weight of 12 would retrieve documents with the following combinations of terms assigned, and these documents or records would be regarded as relevant:

Operator	Search type	Venn diagrams	Meaning
AND	Conjunctive		Logical product, symbolized by A AND B, A, A, B, A × B or (A) (B). Both index terms A and B must be assigned to a document for a match, eg Stage × Lighting × Ballroom / implies that all of the above terms must have been assigned to a document for a match.
OR	Additive		Logical sum, symbolized by A OR B, or A + B. Only one of the two index terms A, or B, need be associated with a document for a match. This operator is usually introduced when A and B can be regarded as equivalent for the purposes of the search, eg Billiards + Snooker / would serve to retrieve all documents with either the term 'Billiards' or the term 'Snooker' assigned.
NOT	Subtractive		Logical difference, symbolized by A NOT B, or A − B. The index term A must be assigned, and assigned in the absence of the term B for a match, eg Ball games − Golf requires all documents on ball games *except* those where 'Golf' is also assigned.

Figure 7.3: Boolean logic operators

Soil and Plants
Soil and Radioisotopes
Soil and Agricultural chemistry
Radioisotopes and Agricultural chemistry
Soil, Food and Agriculture

Documents with the following terms assigned would be rejected on the grounds that their combined weights from each of the terms identified in the records did not exceed the pre-selected threshold:

Productivity and Water
Food and Soil
Radioactive and Agriculture

Weighted-term search logic may also be used to supplement Boolean logic. Here weighted-term logic is a means of limiting or ranking the output from a search that has been conducted with the use of a search profile which was framed in terms of Boolean logic operators. In the search, and prior to display or printing, references or records are ranked according to the weighting that they achieve, and records with sufficiently high rankings will be deemed most relevant, and be selected for display or printing.

In-house text retrieval packages

As mentioned in chapter four, there are special software packages designed to support information or text retrieval. Some of the packages that are used for information retrieval are essentially database-management systems (DBMS), but there are also specially designed text-retrieval packages which offer features appropriate to text retrieval. These packages tend to offer similar facilities to those available on a large international host, although the full range of facilities may not always be available. So, for instance, Ashford lists the following retrieval functions as being provided in nine mainframe and minicomputer systems that he examined:

Boolean query formulation
Search refinement (by sub-questions, etc)
Field or section limits on search scope
File or chapter limits on search scope
Display of 'postings' frequencies
Translation of word terminations
Text 'string' searching

Stored searches or stored questions
Stop lists or 'common word' lists
Synonym recognition
Thesaurus or vocabulary support (except INFOText)
Help for users
Sorting for search results
Editing of search results
Security controls of output at database and field/section level

These may well be taken to characterize text-retrieval packages. The difference between such packages, and the facilities offered by external hosts, is that these packages tend to be implemented by libraries, information units and a wide variety of other organizations in order to manage local databases.

A wide range of possible applications can be identified for such packages, extending well beyond the traditional library and information science fields. ASSASSIN, can, for instance, be used for:

Correspondence	Personnel records
Systems and procedure manuals	Laboratory notes
Personal indexes	Product formulations
Salesman's reports	Newspaper cuttings
Patents records	Market intelligence
Customer files	Catalogues
Medical records	Board minutes

to identify only some of the possible applications.

Packages which support some text-retrieval functions are available on mainframes, minicomputers and microcomputers. Prices range from £50 to around £30,000 or more. Obviously the cheaper, microcomputer-based packages do not offer the same range of facilities as the larger mainframe and mini-computer packages. Some of the cheapest microcomputer packages are database-management systems, rather than purpose-made text-retrieval packages. Nevertheless, these may offer effective retrieval from the smaller database that can be stored on smaller and cheaper microcomputers. In this category might be included Micro-QUERY. EAGLE and CARDBOX. The most expensive microcomputer packages, at, say, a few thousand pounds, do start to offer a wide range of text-retrieval functions on an intermediate-size database.

Figure 7.4: Some text-retrieval packages

Package	*Suppliers*
Mainframe/minicomputer	
ADP/3RIP	ADP Network Services Ltd
ASSASSIN 6	ICI Agricultural Division
BASIS	Battelle Institute Ltd
CAIRS	Leatherhead Food Research Association
DECO	Unilever Computer Services Ltd
DOCU/MASTER	TSI International (UK) Ltd
INFO Text	Doric Computer Systems Ltd
SEARCH	BRS Europe
STATUS	AERE Harwell
Microcomputer	
AQUILA	Kent-Barlow Publications Ltd
CARDBOX	Business Simulations Ltd
EAGLE	Kent-Barlow Publications Ltd
HOMER	Mars Group Services
LIBRARIAN	Eurotec Consultants Ltd
Micro-CAIRS	Leatherhead Food Research Association
Micro-STATUS	AERE Harwell
Micro-QUERY	Advisory Unit for Computer-Based Education

In this category Micro-CAIRS, Micro-STATUS, HOMER and TRS are good examples.

The minicomputer and mainframe packages start in price at between £5,000 and £10,000 and often offer a variety of modules or extra options which may be acquired in order to enhance the facility. In addition to retrieval functions, these packages can also be expected to offer extensive support in the implementation of the package, in the form of manuals, help-desks, training and user groups. These user groups are active in supporting developments of the packages and, in general, examining the application of text retrieval. Two notable groups are the STATUS User Group and the ASSAS-SIN User Club. Other features which are likely to be available in the larger systems include:

a) Some support for running SDI and other current awareness programs;

b) Options in terms of printing and formatting the output (user-defined formats), so that indexes, bibliographies and other listings may be produced in the most acceptable form;

c) Statistical facilities, eg ADD, MEAN, DEVIATION;

d) Novice and experienced user modes;

e) Arrangements for the display of the index.

Further reading
General

East, H 'Comparative costs of manual and online bibliographic searching: a review of the literature'. *Journal of information science* 2(2) September 1980. 101-9.

Deunette, J B *UK online search services.* London, Aslib for Online Information Centre, 1981.

Henry, W M and others *Online searching: an introduction.* London, Butterworths, 1980.

Hoover, R E (ed) *The library and information manager's guide to online services.* White Plains (New York), Knowledge Industry Publications, 1980.

Houghton, B and Convey, J *Online information retrieval systems.* 2nd ed. London, Bingley, 1984.

Lockheed Information Systems *Guide to Dialog databases.* Palo Alto (California), LIS, 1977—.

Meadow, C and Cochrane, P *Basics of online searching.* Chichester, Wiley, 1981.

Negus, A E 'Development of the Euronet Diane Common Command language' in *Proceedings of the 3rd International Online Information Meeting, London, 4th-6th December 1979* Oxford, Learned Information, 1979. 95-8.

Online Information Centre *Going online* (and other publications). London, Online Information Centre, 1983.

Proceedings of the International Online Information Meetings: 5th, 6th, 7th and 8th Oxford, Learned Information, 1981-4.

Wells, C A 'Quick reference command language chart'. *Online Review* 7(1) January 1983, 45-50.

Videotex
Carr, R 'Prestel in the test trial: an academic library user looks back'. *Journal of Librarianship* 12(3) 1980. 145-58.
Lancaster, F W *Towards paperless information systems* New York, Academic Press, 1978.
Martyn, J 'Prestel and public libraries: an LA/Aslib experiment'. *Aslib Proceedings* 31(5) 1979. 216-36.
Plakias, M 'New electronic media: the future and co-operation'. *Reference quarterly,* 20(1) 1980. 66-9.
Shackel, B et al 'The BLEND-LINC project on electronic journals after two years'. *Aslib Proceedings* 35(2) 1982. 77-91.
Singleton, A 'The electronic journal and its relatives'. *Scholarly publishing* 13(1) 1981. 3-18.
Stokes, A V *Viewdata: a public information utility.* Langton Information Systems, 1978.
Yates, D M 'Project HERMES'. *Aslib Proceeedings* 35(4) April 1983. 177-82.
Yeates, R *A librarian's introduction to private viewdata systems* London, LASER, 1982.

In-house text-retrieval packages
Ashford, J 'Information storage and retrieval systems on mainframes and minicomputers: a comparison of text retrieval packages available in the UK'. *Program* 18(2) April 1984. 124-46.
Ashford, J and Matkin, D *Studies in the application of free text package systems* London, LA, 1982. (Case Studies in Library Automation).
Kimberley, R et al *Software for text retrieval: a directory.* London, Gower for the Institute of Information Scientists, 1984.
'Program: special issue on software packages for information retrieval'. *Program* 16(3) July 1982.
Williams H L (ed) *Computerised systems in library and information sciences* London, Aslib, 1983.

Chapter Eight

Current awareness services

Current awareness services are those information services whose primary intent is to keep information users alert to advances in their field. Any current awareness service involves collecting surrogates of recent literature and other data and grouping them in a manner that makes it possible to dispatch relevant notifications to a group of users.

The scale of the operation may vary both in terms of the number of users served and the volume of literature or data handled. At one extreme, large services such as BIOSIS and INSPEC are selling services to an international audience across a broad discipline; whilst at the other, small company information units such as Cadburys or the West Midlands Area Health Authority may be serving only a few hundred users in a relatively narrow and well-defined subject. Nevertheless, all current awareness services share two features which make them an exposed target for computerization.

a) The size of the files (eg number of citations) involved is relatively small since the files appertain to a short time span;

b) Current awareness services are acceptable in 'batch mode'. With current awareness services users' interest descriptions can be refined over a series of trial runs (see Figure 8.1).

A computerized information system opens a number of possibilities with respect to current awareness services. One of the most significant innovations in this field is the very much more sophisticated SDI programmes. SDI is not generally regarded as feasible on any scale, ie to any number of users, without the support of a computer. The other value of the computer in the production of current awareness services

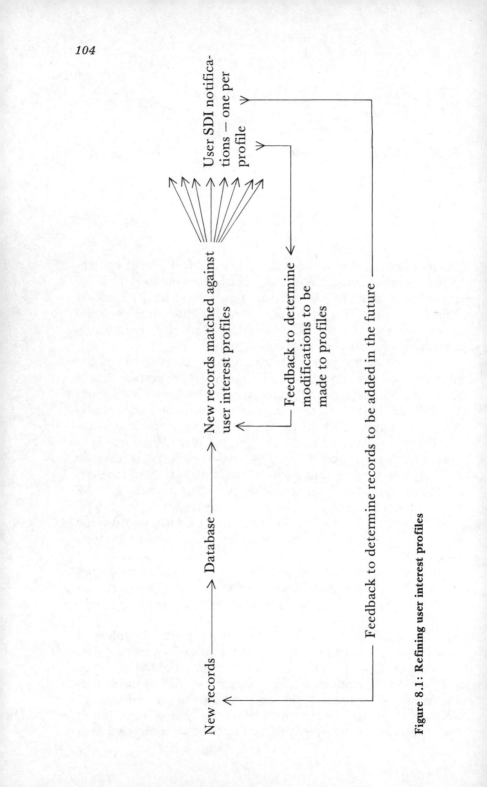

Figure 8.1: Refining user interest profiles

is the wide range of such services that can be derived from one database, thus making it possible to offer services which suit a large number of different approaches to information gathering and current awareness and make services available for different pockets.

Selective Dissemination of Information (SDI)

As originally perceived by H P Luhn, every document entering an SDI system would be abstracted and assigned a coded document pattern, based on about forty keywords taken from the text. Each document is then matched against a pattern of terms encapsulating a user's interests (a profile) and a notification sent to the user if the (weighted) proportion of codes in the document pattern which matched those in the profile exceeded a predetermined threshold. Profiles were to be updated by studying the requests received for complete documents from the user.

In other words, SDI is a current awareness mechanism through which the individual information user can expect to receive regular notifications of new literature and data in accordance with his statement of interests or profile. All SDI systems take their inspiration from Luhn, but do not always adhere precisely to the terms of his definition.

Keywords may be drawn from any field, including authors' names, titles, chemical names, journal titles, and the text of an abstract or a document. Also, keywords may be either more or less numerous than in Luhn's definition.

SDI producers

The first step towards the use of an SDI service is the identification of the source of such services. There are four main groups of SDI providers: local library and information services, large database producers and processors, national libraries, and online hosts.

Most of the local libraries which generate SDI services will do so with the aid of one of the software packages specifically designed for text retrieval, which have been introduced in the previous chapter. Many larger industrial and other special libraries create their own database and generate current awareness services from that database, each time that the database is updated. Most software packages which offer any form of text retrieval can be used for current awareness, merely by the user consulting the database at regular intervals, as and when the database is updated.

The most basic option in support of an SDI service is the possibility of saving a search profile so that it may be executed again at a later date. Obviously it is extremely tedious to have to re-enter a search profile each time that a specific search profile needs to be executed. Obviously too it is an advantage if the package supports the storage of not one but several such profiles. A further simple facility which supports easy SDI is the ability to obtain regular outputs by selection on date ranges (in order to identify records that have been entered recently).

Thus most packages, even the smaller microcomputer packages, can offer rudimentary current awareness facilities if the user has access to a terminal on which he can search the database, and has the expertise for searching the database. The more sophisticated text-retrieval packages offer a more comprehensive range of facilities to support current awareness services. Packages such as CAIRS and ASSA3SIN will have the facilities to support the processing of a large number of SDI profiles in either batch or online mode on a regular basis, usually each time that the file is updated. Although a user may have the option of viewing notifications at a terminal most of these larger packages support the printing of groups of notifications, and their dispatch to the person for whom a specific profile has been constructed. In order to support this process, it is useful if the package offers the possibility of the user defining the format of the printed output. Selection of the elements to be printed can be expected to be restricted by the date that the records entered the system, the file in which records are contained, specified records, and specified fields within records. For larger print-outs features such as page formatting, choice of typefaces and page numbering can also be useful. The ability to store and print names and addresses for use in the dispatch of SDI notifications is also valuable.

The records which can be searched by local libraries may vary from one institution to another. Some organizations have databases which relate entirely to local documents, eg internal reports, correspondence, etc, whereas others include information and bibliographical references which are publicly available. Some of the records in local databases are bibliographic in nature, whilst others are records of actual information or data. Where the database contains publicly available information, the records, especially if they are bibliographic records, may be created by the information service concerned, or may be derived from other externally available databases, either by lease or purchase of magnetic tapes, or by downloading from one of the databases accessible through one of the online hosts.

SDI is also available direct from the large database producers and suppliers. Some such services are:

SDI	Database	Supplier
ASCA	*Science, social sciences, arts and humanities citation indexes*	Institute for Scientific Information
COMPENDEX	COMPENDEX	Engineering Information Inc
DRUGDOC	DRUGDOC	Excerpta Medica
INSPEC SDI	INSPEC	Institution of Electrical Engineers
Weldasearch System 1	*Welding abstracts*	Welding Institute

The third major group of suppliers of SDI services are the national libraries of some countries. CAN/SDI is a national SDI service based on around twenty databases encompassing agriculture, biology, chemistry, medicine, social sciences, education, science and technology, etc. Initiated by the Canada Institute for Scientific and Technical Information, CAN/SDI is now run cooperatively by six centres, and users are to be found in industry, universities, government and hospitals throughout Canada and, to a lesser extent, in the United States and other countries. Australia, Belgium and Denmark also run SDI programs from the national library. There are further centres that have a special responsibility with respect to SDI. UKCIS (originally the United Kingdom Chemical Information Service) was established to offer SDI services and other computer-based information-retrieval services in chemistry and biology.

The British Library has responsibility for an SDI service derived from the MEDLARS database (produced by the National Library of Medicine). The Royal Institute of Technology in Stockholm operates a service similar in scale to CAN/SDI and the University of Georgia also maintains a large number of profiles.

The fourth category of producers of SDI are the online hosts. An SDI facility has been introduced by most of the major hosts over the past few years. Dialog, ORBIT and INFOLINE all offer this facility. As with a local database, SDI can obviously be gleaned by a diligent user by re-running a search profile at intervals in order to check whether any new items have been retrieved. Most hosts offer a command which permits profiles to be saved, and some offer a special facility for SDI which ensures that if a profile is saved as an SDI profile, then the profile will be run every time that the database is updated (say monthly). If the profile contains a command to create offline prints, then a set of offline prints will be created each time that the profile is run against a new batch of records, and this set will be dispatched to the user. This type of facility is available for many of the databases which are searchable through the online hosts, but usually not all of the databases of any given host.

Profiles
The user-interest profile is the core of any SDI system. Profile construction may be in the hands of the end-user, his librarian or other intermediary, or a specialist employed by the service vendor. Effective profile compilation demands familiarity with both the subject and the database. Generally the user has precise notions about what he would like from the service and a database specialist understands the system, but neither can hope to be fully conversant with both. CAN/SDI delegates profiling to local search editors, eg the local librarian, backed by checking at the search centre. A librarian trained in the system and geographically close to the user, is in a good position to discuss his information requirements. Consultation on profile formulation has been found to give the best results.

Profiles are based on the user's statement of his interests. This statement, which may be entered on a profile search form like that shown in Figure 8.2, usually specifies: a) the topics to be covered; b) keywords pertinent to those topics; and c) ten or so titles of known relevant papers. This data is then used to construct the more formal search profile. A search profile comprises: a) a list of terms representing the user's interests, in the language of the database to be searched; and b) a statement of the logical conditions required for a match and the printing of a notification.

The quality of the profile and its success in accurately mirroring the user's interests are crucial to the value of the output from an SDI system. The most appropriate design for a profile depends on the database, the mode of access (batch or online) and the user's attitude to irrelevant items (ie whether he seeks high recall or high precision).

Profile formulation starts with the identification of subject concepts and their expression as keywords. As in retrospective searching keywords can include any terms or combinations of terms that are machine-searchable, such as authors' names, subject terms, title words, chemical formulae, journal titles and dates.

The next stage is to introduce the logical conditions to be satisfied for a hit. This is usually achieved using Boolean logic operators. The basic Boolean operators may be used in conjunction with contextual logic operators, truncation, and other search facilities for framing search statements which contribute to an SDI profile, in a similar way to that evident in online searching. These topics have already been explored in chapter seven. Figure 8.3 gives a further example of search statements and a profile as it might be found in an SDI service.

Although in principle and general structure a search statement for current awareness profiles has much in common with a search statement for a retrospective search there are some differences. These might be listed as:

1   SDI profiles are likely to be less specific, since the quantity of new information which is likely to become available, over say, one week or one month, is in most instances likely to be very much less than the cumulated knowledge on the subject field. Thus, since the quantity of information being searched is less, an SDI profile can afford to be somewhat wider without overwhelming the reader with an excessive number of items. Conversely, if the SDI profile is too narrow items may only be retrieved relatively rarely, and it may be difficult to justify the continuation of the service (if nothing new has been produced for some months, then the user may question what he is paying for).

2   SDI profiles are possibly more likely to be regularly matched against several databases, rather than merely searching one or two.

3   An SDI profile can be refined over a greater number of

BIOSIS INFORMATION TRANSFER SYSTEM (B-I-T-S^{TM})

PROFILE DEVELOPMENT FORM

Name_____

Title_____

Organization_____

Address_____

City_____State_____Zip_____

Telephone_____/_____

Micro (Name)_____Disk Size(K)_____

Operating System_____

Instructions: This profile development form has been designed to record subject selection criteria for your B-I-T-S subscription. No experience with the BIOSIS indexing system is required.

1. GENERAL REQUIREMENTS-IN THE SPACE BELOW, WRITE A BRIEF DESCRIPTION OF THE KIND OF INFORMATION (REFERENCES) YOU WANT TO RECEIVE.

_____
_____
_____
_____
_____
_____
_____

2. SUBJECT AREAS-USING THE ENCLOSED LIST OF SUBJECT AREAS, CHOOSE ONE OR TWO THAT DESCRIBE YOUR OVERALL AREAS OF INTEREST. USE THE NUMBERS TO THE RIGHT OF EACH TOPIC AND WRITE THEM IN THE BOXES.

3. SPECIFIC TERMS-IN THE SPACES BELOW WRITE THE SPECIFIC TERMS (NAMES OF DISEASES, DRUGS, INSTRUMENTS ETC.) THAT WILL HELP US SELECT DOCUMENTS FOR YOUR PROFILE. IN THE SPACE PROVIDED INDICATE IF THE TERM IS (C) CRITICAL, (I) IMPORTANT, (U) USEFUL.

C-I-U	TERM		C-I-U	TERM		C-I-U	TERM

Figure 8.2

4. ORGANISMS-USING THE SPACES BELOW PROVIDE THE NAME(S) OF ANY ORGANISMS (INCLUDING MAN) THAT YOU WANT INCLUDED. USE SCIENTIFIC NAMES IF POSSIBLE. YOU MAY USE ANY TAXONOMIC LEVEL (CLASS, ORDER, FAMILY, GENUS). USE THE SPACE PROVIDED TO INDICATE IMPORTANCE OF THE ORGANISM AS YOU DID IN 3 ABOVE. (THIS AREA MAY BE LEFT BLANK).

C-I-U	ORGANISM		C-I-U	ORGANISM

5. THE NUMBER OF ITEMS SELECTED IN RESPONSE TO THIS PROFILE SHOULD BE NO MORE THAN _____ ANNUALLY.

6. MY B-I-T-S SUBSCRIPTION SHOULD INCLUDE:

____REFERENCES ONLY
____REFERENCES & AVAILABLE ABSTRACTS

_____
(Signature)

RETURN TO: BIOSIS USER SERVICES, 2100 ARCH STREET, PA 19103-1399
- -
FOR BIOSIS USE ONLY:

B-I-T-S ESTIMATES

THE ANNUAL NUMBER OF B-I-T-S ITEMS FROM THIS PROFILE WILL BE APPROXIMATELY:_____

_____REFERENCES ONLY

_____REFERENCES WITH ABSTRACTS

_____
Systems Design & Development
Staff Authorization

Figure 8.2 continued

```
? b 40
            17may83 11:20:37 User3842
    $0.08  0.003 Hrs File1*
    $0.02  Uninet
    $0.10  Estimated Total Cost


File40:ENVIROLINE - 71-83/June
(Copr. EIC Inc.)
            Set Items Description
            --- ----- -----------
? ss (wood? or firewood) and (heat? or stove? or combust? or smoke?)
            1    939 WOOD?
            2     85 FIREWOOD
            3   2402 HEAT?
            4     40 STOVE?
            5   1738 COMBUST?
            6    697 SMOKE?
            7    100 (1 OR 2) AND (3 OR 4 OR 5 OR 6)
? t 7/8/1-2
7/8/1
    160488  *82-006147
    1981 OREGON  AIR  QUALITY ANNUAL REPORT:  WOOD HEATING AND AIR
QUALITY,
    DESCRIPTORS: *OREGON ;  *AIR QUALITY CRITERIA ;   *FIREWOOD ;
SPACE HEATING, DOMESTIC ;  *STACK EMISSIONS ;  *DATA, ENV-AIR ;
*MONITORING, ENV-AIR ;  *AIR QUALITY PROGRAMS ;   *AIR QUALITY
STANDS, AMBIENT ; OPEN BURNING ; PARTICULATES ;  URBAN ATMOSPHERE
; CARBON MONOXIDE ; OZONE
    REVIEW CLASSIFICATION: 01


7/8/2
    159003  *82-004687
    DROPPING ACID: ACID RAIN,
    DESCRIPTORS:  *ACID RAIN ;   *AIR POLLUTION RESEARCH ;  *AIR
POLLUTION  EFFECTS  ;   *POWER  PLANTS-COAL  FIRED  ;   *LAKES ;
*TRANSNATIONAL POLLUTION ; LIME
    REVIEW CLASSIFICATION: 01
```

> Searcher enters "dummy"
> PRINT command, specifying
> maximum number of records
> per update

```
? pr 7/5/1-25
Printed7/5/1-25  Estimated Cost: $6.25 (To cancel, enter PR-)
? end/sdi
Serial#B91T
            17may83 11:22:42 User3842
    $3.24  0.036 Hrs File40 6 Descriptors
    $0.22  Uninet
    $3.46  Estimated Total Cost
```

> SDI established with
> END/SDI command

> Retrospective search
> results PRINTed

```
? pr 7/5/1-100
Printed7/5/1-100  Estimated Cost: $25.00 (To cancel, enter PR-)
? logoff
            17may83 11:23:07 User3842
    $0.72  0.008 Hrs File40
    $0.05  Uninet
    $25.00 100 Prints
    $25.77 Estimated Total Cost


LOGOFF 11:23:10                                            69
```

Figure 8.3: SDI profiles using DIALOG

searches. The profile, is, for instance, likely to be operated in a similar form for many months, or even years. This means that if the profile is not entirely successful immediately, or if the user has not accurately communicated his needs to the profiler, there is the opportunity to rectify this situation against new sets of documents as the months pass (see figure 8.1 above). This scope for refining SDI profiles makes it more likely that an SDI profile, after some months, will be more accurately reflecting the user's needs than a profile used in an online search for retrospective material.

4 Much SDI processing is still in batch mode. In this situation the profile is frequently largely evolved and established before the information on which the searches will eventually be conducted is available. The profile may well be prepared in advance of the publication of some of the material to which it will be applied, and it may be difficult to predict new developments. Even online profile evolution and amendment, which helps to avoid synonyms and related terms being overlooked, may not entirely eradicate this problem.

Output
The outcome of an SDI run will be a series of document records. Where the database which has been searched is bibliographic, the output will be a series of unique sets of references, with one set of references for each profile. Bibliographic references from an SDI run may give the complete record contained in the database, or only some fields from the record. Thus some options might be to print reference numbers only (assuming that the complete record can be identified in some other source, printed or online), full bibliographic citation, including, say, a title but not an abstract, the full record, or just the titles of the records. Output may be printed on line print-out continuous stationery or on a pack of cards with one card per reference or record, or may be made available for viewing at a terminal. Figures 8.3 and 8.4 show some records from an SDI output.

As with all current awareness services, so with SDI successful operation depends on some mechanism for follow-up. The user must have a channel for obtaining copies of the original document, if a bibliographic database has been searched, and for expresssing his opinions regarding the acceptability of the SDI output. These two channels may be very similar if SDI is

Welding [of iron castings].   *102615
WALTON C F; OPAR T J; IRON CASTINGS SOCIETY INC
In: Iron Castings Handbook. 3rd Edition. Eds: C.F.Walton and T.J.Opar. Publ:
Rocky River, OH 44116, USA; Iron Castings Society; 1981. Chapter 11. pp.599-
665. 42 fig., 14 tab., 27 ref.
[in English]

A review is given of the welding of iron castings for assembly, repair,
reclamation and surfacing. Aspects covered include: compositions of MMA
electrodes; factors influencing weld quality; microstructures of fusion zone
and HAZ; stresses due to welding; cracking; joint preparation; preheating;
cooling rate; gas metal arc welding; flux cored arc welding; buttering;
tensile, toughness and hardness properties of welds; oxyacetylene welding;
powder welding; braze welding; thermit welding; fusion casting of iron to
steel; bimetallic casting; flash welding; gas and arc surfacing; flame
spraying; brazing; soldering; gas cutting; arc cutting.

**Figure 8.4: One record from a set of notifications issued in response to
a Weldasearch 1 profile run by the Welding Institute**

being provided within an organization, but may differ if the
SDI service is provided by, say, a database producer, and the
supply of documents is undertaken by a local, or perhaps
national library. Online ordering and document-delivery systems are improving and are an area into which a number of
research projects are being directed. Particularly in connection
with an online SDI service it is possible to order documents
whilst still at the terminal. Indeed, this may be regarded as
one of the strengths of an online SDI service. However, ordering does not constitute supply, and except where facilities
like facsimile transmission coupled with the computer storage
of the full text of a document are available at an acceptable
cost, document delivery is still by post. Online ordering, does,
however, generate useful statistics concerning the requests for
documents which can be put to good use in assessing the
effectiveness of the profile, and a detailed analysis could
indicate the aspects of the profile that are at fault or which
do not generate as many relevant references as might be
expected. Where online ordering is not operational, monitor-
ing the requests placed for documents which have been
notified in an SDI output is still a valuable means of assessing
the effectiveness of the SDI service, but collecting statistics
and analysing them may be more labour intensive.

Feedback is especially necessary after the first three or four
batches of output, so that the profile may be assessed. These
first few batches on a new profile with a new user are often
regarded as experimental and extensive profile refinements
may be necessary before an established profile is achieved.
After this initial period, a regular review cycle, of, say, once a

year, is good practice in order to guarantee that profiles keep abreast of changes in users' interests.

Online vs batch SDI

In online SDI a profile is stored and run, usually specifically at the user's instigation, as required. The profile may also be run on a regular basis, say, at monthly intervals. Online SDI has advantages over batch SDI, but is unlikely to oust batch SDI altogether.

Online SDI offers flexibility in print-out, and, as with online retrospective searching, permits the user to view and select references or records at the terminal, prior to printing relevant items. Extra bonuses also accrue if online notification can be followed by online ordering of the documents if the database being searched is bibliographic in nature.

It is difficult to make a direct cost comparison between online and batch SDI, because costs will vary between applications and neither option is universally cheaper. Costs depend upon the number of references retrieved, the breadth of the profile (number of concepts included), and the frequency of the output, amongst other factors.

Batch SDI is likely to retain some followers because it is convenient, and requires minimal effort on the part of the user. The main advantage of online operation, the possibility for interactive searching and profile development, is not especially important in SDI, except in the initial stages. The disadvantage of online SDI is that the onus is on the user to think about collecting the SDI notifications on a regular basis, whereas with batch operations print-out will appear at regular intervals without any thought on the part of the user. Further, in order to glean the notifications in an online SDI service, the user has to have ready access to terminals. This is less of a problem if users normally have access to terminals for other parts of their work, such as the consultation of an inhouse database, or in retrospective searching of international hosts, but still remains a barrier for some users. Thus, even the online hosts generally support SDI services which allow online profile formulation and modification, but offline notification, in the form of printed notifications.

The computer and other current awareness services

Most libraries and database producers find that to exploit effort directed towards database compilation and refinement, it is desirable to be able to re-package the basic ingredients of their database in as many different formats as have some market. Libraries and information units are often concerned to meet the information requirements of discrete user groups such as research scientists, marketing personnel and factory management, within the framework of one information system. Commercial database producers likewise wish to market their product to a wide audience. One of the chief advantages of a computerized information-retrieval system is the ability to draw a range of tailored products from one database. In the province of current awareness services, this has led to services suited to the individual, to groups and to libraries.

SDI has significantly advanced the service to the individual. However, at prices of around £150 or more for one profile for a year, individual SDI may be regarded as prohibitively expensive. Two common solutions are Group SDI and Standard SDI.

Group SDI, as the name implies, is geared towards the interests of a group of individuals such as a research and development department, or a university teaching team. In general, a group SDI profile is less specific than an individual profile and, in addition to spreading the cost of the service, widens the field of which the individual is kept aware. A broader profile may be regarded as beneficial or time-wasting, depending on the nature and philosophy of the user group. Local information systems may generate print-outs according to departmental or divisional interests; such print-outs are equivalent to a series of bulletins, and may be regarded as such.

Commercial database processors have also exploited the similarity of some SDI profiles. Standard SDI programs are based on a series of pre-set profiles covering a number of standard subjects or topics. As well as being cheaper to generate, and hence buy, standard SDI eliminates much local profile evaluation and formulation. Standard SDI is thus much easier to use, provided that an appropriate subject is available. Output is in card form, or on continuous paper print-out, or in bulletin format. Examples of standard SDI are:

Weldasearch System 2, from the Welding Institute Topics, from the Institution of Electrical Engineers

ASCA Topics, from the Institute for Scientific Information

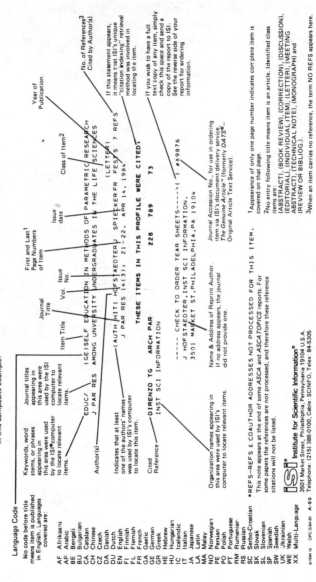

Figure 8.5: One record from ASCATOPICS

SIPS (Selected Information Profiles Service), from BHRA Fluid Engineering Centre

BIOSIS Standard Profiles, from Biosciences Information Services and, produced on disk rather than printed:

MICRO/B-I-T-S and MACRO/B-I-T-S, from Biosciences Information Services.

In addition to standard SDI, some database producers also market rather broader bulletins, whose format is more suited to library control and exploitation. INSPEC's *Key abstracts,* a series of titles covering areas such as electronic circuits, systems theory, and solid state devices, containing around two hundred abstracts each month, fall into this category.

The abstracting or indexing journal is the database producer's primary library-oriented product. These publications remain an important component of any information product range. The abstracting or indexing journal or bulletin is the most economic tool for providing large numbers of users with a reference-retrieval service. The basic objectives of such services have changed little with mechanization. It is not our intention here to review the role and objectives of abstracting and indexing journals, but to comment on the impact of computerization. The computer is efficient at arranging, sorting, cumulating and printing. The production of a large abstracting journal involves many of these tasks. Advanced computer-printing techniques have made the printing of publications easier and more economic. The ease of rearrangement of citations has permitted an array of abstracting journals to be derived from a single database, as with *Excerpta medica.* Mechanization has improved the standard of index provision. Cumulative indexes were once only available annually and then, all too frequently, well after the completion of the volume. Now many are issued quarterly, with annual, five-yearly and ten-yearly cumulations, and the variety of index types has been expanded.

Examples

Infoline
SDI can be operated on all Infoline files. It is designed so that a search profile can be created online, and then re-run automatically to produce offline SDI notifications, which arrive at the user's address with no additional intervention on the

part of the user. This can be achieved by using the P SAVE routine to save a search once it has been run so that the search profile may be re-run as an SDI search, or by using P MAKE in INFO which is a cheap method of creating a strategy without simultaneously running the search. A strategy for a profile for SDI must contain an offline print command, and appropriately constructed this will mean that every time that the database on which the SDI is to be run is updated (say monthly) a set of offline prints will be created. This service costs £2 to £3 per update, plus the normal offline print prices for the database used.

Dialog

SDI search formulations can be stored permanently with the END/SDI command. Such a search is shown in Figure 8.3. These formulations may be released by the user when it is convenient. The charges for this service depend upon the database being used and the number of offline prints that are selected as a result of running the profile. The routine running of saved search profiles is available on 47 files. In order to ensure printing of notifications a PRINT command must be included in all SDI profiles.

SCICON

SCICON is a host responsible for providing access to:

 a) POLIS which covers parliamentary information, legislation and official publications;

 b) ACOMPLINE which covers urban policies and development from the Research Library of the Greater London Council

 c) URBALINE which covers urban and local government issues, and

 d) DHSS-DATA, which covers information on health and the social sciences, from the Department of Health and Social Security.

 SDI search profiles can be stored, at £1 per month, and run against any of the databases at the user's convenience. Output can be either printed on the user's own terminal, or on Scicon's line printers and posted to the user. Aslib has been authorized to conduct searches, including SDI searches, for non-ACOMPLINE users against this database.

PIRA

PIRA, the Research Association for the Paper and Board, Printing and Package Industries, monitors and stores technical, commercial and legislative information in order to generate five industry-tailored information services. These are: *Electronic publishing abstracts*, *Printing abstracts*, *Paper and board abstracts*, *International packaging abstracts*, and *Management and marketing abstracts*. The databases associated with each of these services are mounted by Pergamon-Infoline. The current awareness services that are derived from the databases are integrated into a fully supported programme of library and information services. In addition to online searching, back-up facilities include full text retrieval, a translation service, magnetic tape leasing, and manual searches. The same range of current awareness services is offered on all databases, with the exception of *Management and marketing abstracts*. For example, in respect of *Electronic publishing abstracts* the following current awareness services are available:

a) *Abstracts journal,* a printed and indexed monthly publication. Each issue contains nearly 250 references, covering topics such as: retrieval systems, output, CAD, input, communications, storage. Various prices apply, but the 1984 annual subscription in the UK for non-members is £150.

b) *Advance abstracts service*, a bi-weekly current awareness print-out providing the same information as the journal, but issuing the abstracts in computer print-out form. By this means, information is received at least four weeks earlier than with option a). Again, various prices apply, but the 1984 annual subscription in the UK for non-members is £150.

c) *Standard topic profiles* are a range of standard profiles offering coverage of 18 different topics, including technological and economic trends, health and safety, word processing, cable TV, etc. Various prices apply, but the 1984 annual subscription in the UK for non-members is £92.50 for one topic and increases according to the number of topics required, eg three topics are £184.50.

d) *Personal information profiles* are available to cover several different categories of abstract or database. These are updated and despatched bi-weekly. Various prices apply, but the 1984 annual subscription in the UK for non-members is £150 upwards.

INSPEC

INSPEC publishes three abstracts journals: *Computer and control abstracts, Electrical and electronics abstracts,* and *Physics abstracts*. These journals together with *IT focus* which is mentioned below contain all of the information which is entered into the INSPEC database. In addition to these abstracts journals and their associated database, INSPEC markets a number of current awareness services. These include:

a) *IT focus* for the business manager and executive covering all aspects of IT and the automated office. Some 400 abstracts are included each year and the journal is published monthly, with an annual index. The UK 1984 price is £70.

b) *Current papers* for scientists and engineers in the three areas covered by the services: *Current papers in physics, Current papers in electrical and electronics engineering,* and *Current papers on computers and control. Current papers* provide the titles of articles and details of the source documents for rapid current awareness. With the exception of *Current papers in physics,* which is published twice a month, the other services are published monthly. Articles are arranged by subject but no indexes are provided. Prices vary, but for example, the 1984 UK non-member annual subscription for *Current papers in computers and control* is £88.

c) *Key abstracts* select information from only the more important journals and conference proceedings and provide short summaries. *Key abstracts* are published as eight separate journals, covering, for instance: Power transmission and distribution, Communication technology, and Systems theory. *Key abstracts* are published monthly. The 1984 UK annual subscription for a non-member to each journal is £40.

d) *SDI*: a tailored service which matches the profile of the user against the information added to the INSPEC database each week. Profiles may be changed at any time in order to improve the effectiveness of the selection. Each week the subscriber receives a set of notification cards, and each card includes title, reference, and a truncated abstract. The service is weekly and prices start from £165 (UK, 1984).

e) *Topics* are a set of standard SDI profiles. Each week the subscriber receives a set of selected notification cards giving the same information as in the SDI option. Some examples of topics coverage include: Amorphous semiconductors,

Switchgear, Pattern recognition, and Automatic testing. The price during 1984 for a UK subscriber is £65 per topic.

f) *INSPEC online:* the INSPEC database is accessible through a number of the major hosts, including BRS, Data-Star, SDC and Dialog. Many of these hosts offer the possibility of running an SDI profile against the databases which they have mounted.

The electronic journal

The electronic journal is a rather different approach to current awareness. With teleconferencing and the availability of various compilations of data and text online, the natural proposal is for an electronic journal, which makes use of telecommunications networks and computer storage to enable scientists and others to interact and communicate research in a new technology-based mode. Thus the electronic journal is a concept where scientists are able to input ideas and text to a computer database for their colleagues to view, and similarly to view the work of others. Various modes of operation are possible for such a journal, and the precise operation will depend upon the type of information being conveyed. Some possibilities are: chit-chat, work messages, news about the electronic journal network, an enquiry-answer system between experts, a bulletin, an annotated abstracts journal, discussion and questions on papers, a poster-papers journal and a refereed-papers journal. These options obviously range from the very informal to the very formal.

Two major projects in this area have been conducted to date. The first electronic journal was established with funding from the National Science Foundation on the EIES network and ran from 1976 to 1980. More recently, the BLEND project was established by the British Library as a cooperative effort between Birmingham University and Loughborough University. The topic of the journal is Computer human factors. This started in 1980, and has around 40 members who receive some support to cover telephone charges. The journal is a traditional refereed journal. So contributions are input to the database, then refereed, ie suggestions are made by the referee through the database for improvement; these suggestions can be picked up by the editor, and communication can continue through the same medium until eventually the paper is accepted. This process has the advantage of retaining the refereeing and editing processes whilst streamlining communication, and removing the need for the costly stages of journal production such as printing, publishing, marketing and distribution. When the basic feasibility and desirability of the electronic journal has been assessed it will be necessary to consider the organization and indexing of contributions in these journals, and the bibliographic control of such journals. However, it must be stressed that these problems are still in the future.

Further reading

Housmann, E M 'Selective dissemination of information'. *Annual review of information science and technology* 8 1973. 221-41.

Kemp, A *Current awareness services.* London, Bingley, 1979. (Outlines of modern librarianship)

Leggate, P 'Computer-based current awareness services'. *Journal of documentation* 31(2) 1975. 93-115.

Rowley, J E and Turner, C M D *The dissemination of information.* London, Deutsch, 1978.

Chapter Nine

Printed indexes

One of the first applications of computers in information retrieval was in the production of printed indexes. Computers were used both for in-house indexes to reports lists, local abstracting and indexing bulletins, patents lists, etc and for the production of published indexes to many of the major abstracting journals. Particularly for the large abstracting and indexing organizations, computerization of indexes and indexing yielded considerable savings in the production and cumulation of indexes. Originally index production was an isolated operation. Now, many indexes are merely one of a range of products derived from a computer-held bibliographic database. In order to focus attention on the effect of the computer on indexing, and printed indexes, they are here treated in their own right.

In spite of the growth of online retrospective searching, for some time yet there will be searches in which reference to a printed index is cheaper and simpler. Several different access points may be used in printed indexes. The most important of these are subject and author; but chemical formulae, trade names, company names and patent numbers are all possible access points.

All indexes consist of a series of lead terms, arranged usually in alphabetical order. Each lead term may be qualified and must have a link that leads the user to other lists or documents. A one-stage index has a link which gives sufficient bibliographic details to locate the original document, eg full journal reference for a journal article. A link in a two-stage index merely directs to another listing, where fuller details of the original document are usually to be found.

Most indexes are geared to retrospective searching, but a

simple machine-produced index can also be an invaluable current awareness tool, provided that reasonably complete citations are available. Indeed, the first machine-based index created by H P Luhn, and listing titles of articles appearing in *Chemical abstracts* in 1961, was intended primarily as a current awareness tool.

Computer-generated indexes may be online printer print-out or may be formatted and reduced, or may be printed with the aid of photocomposition. When paper printout becomes too bulky or expensive, microfilm or microfiche can be used.

Computer-generated indexes may rely on machine-assigned index terms or intellectually-assigned terms. Each of these possibilities will now be considered.

KWIC, KWOC, KWIT and KWAC

A KWIC (Keyword-in-Context) index is the most basic of natural language indexes, and is widely used in in-house applications. Natural language indexing depends on 'terms in text'. Terms can be selected from the text manually, but most natural language indexing is based on machine-selection of terms from a title, or other field of a bibliographic record, such as the abstract.

KWIC or KWIT (Keyword-in-Title) indexes are popular because they are straightforward and relatively cheap to create; standard program packages are readily available. To name but a few examples, KWIC indexes and their variants are produced by IBM as a report index, the Nuclear Safety Information Center as indexes to bibliographies, ASSASSIN as indexes to abstracting bulletins and the like and Bath University Library as an index to their catalogue.

In the most basic of KWIC indexes, words in a title are compared with a stop-list, in order to suppress the generation of useless index entries. The stop-list or stopword-list contains words under which entries are not required, such as: them, his, her, other, and. Each word in the title is compared with those in the stop-list and if a match occurs it is rejected; but if no match is found, the term is designated a keyword. These keywords are used as entry words, with one entry relating to the document for each word. The word is printed in context with the remainder of the title (including stopwords). Entry words are arranged alphabetically and aligned in the centre

the professions./The effect of	language	on social mobility in	059606
of Esperanto./	Language	awareness and the place	06355
fisheries periodical literature./	Language	use patterns in the	07921
trends of international activities in	languages./	A report on the present	05555
The use of command	languages	in online information retrieval./	07341
Indexing	languages:	some dilemmas./	06781
Who's who in special	libraries./		04431
	Libraries	and the MARC format./	05423
communications networks for	libraries./	Electronic mail systems:	05609
Use of systems programs in	library	applications of microcomputers./	06782
The structure and dynamics of	library	services./	04612

Figure 9.1: An example of a KWIC index layout

or left column. A single line entry, including title and source reference, is produced for each signficant word in the title. The source reference frequently amounts to no more than a document or abstract number, but may extend to an abbreviated journal citation. Alternatively, a full bibliographic description, with or without abstract, can be located in a separate listing. Entries under one word are arranged alphabetically by title, as in the example.

The merits of title indexes derive mainly from the low human intervention. Since a simple KWIC index is entirely machine-generated, a large number of titles can be processed quickly and cheaply. The elimination of personal interpretation enhances consistency and predictability. Indexing based on words in titles reflects current terminology, automatically evolving with the use of the terminology. With machine processing, cumulation is easier and does not demand any added effort, only an extra computer run.

However, for all their convenience, title indexes are open to criticism on the following several counts:

a) Titles do not accurately mirror the content of a document. Titles can always be found which are misleading or eye-catching rather than informative, eg 'The Black-white divide (politics or graphics?)'. Titles are becoming more informative, but there will always remain serious limitations on the amount of information that a title can convey.

b) Basic KWIC indexes are unattractive and uncomfortable to read, due to their physical arrangement and typeface. Keywords can be difficult to identify and the remainder of the title may be truncated or difficult to place in the proper sequence. If a title exceeds the allocated line length, it will be indiscriminately cut. Computer print-out, depending upon its form, can be tiring to scan.

c) Sub-arrangement at entry terms would also improve the scannability and searchability of KWIC indexes, by breaking down long sequences of entries under the same keyword; alphabetical sub-arrangement is dictated by the accident of the structure of the title.

d) The remainder of the criticisms of title indexes are concerned with the absence of terminology control. Irrelevant and redundant entries are inevitable. The mere appearance of a term in a title does not necessarily herald the treatment of a topic at any length in the body of the text. Further, even

Language

The effect of * on social mobility in the professions   059606

* awareness and the place of Esperanto   06355

* use patterns in the fisheries periodical literature   07921

Languages

A report on the present trends of international activities in *   05555

The use of command * in online information retrieval   07341

Indexing * some dilemmas   06781

Libraries

Who's who in special *   04431

* and the MARC format   05423

Electronic mail systems: communications networks for *   05609

Library

An investigation of the use of systems programs in * applications of microcomputer   06782

The structure and dynamics of * services   04612

when the term assigned is relevant, with no terminology control, all the problems, which a controlled language aims to counter, re-emerge. Subjects will be scattered under a variety of terms with similar meanings. No directions are inserted between related subjects.

The more sophisticated KWIC-type programs attempt to negotiate these four limitations. Readability can be improved by simply altering the printed format. A KWOC (Keyword-out-of-Context) index, for instance, extracts the keyword from the title; the keyword is used as a separate heading, with titles and accession numbers listed beneath it. An asterisk sometimes replaces the keyword in the printed title. Indexes where the keyword appears both as heading and in the title are strictly KWAC indexes (Keyword-and-Context), but this distinction is rarely made, and KWOC is the generic term used. KWOC indexes appear superficially like a conventional subject index. Other, simpler means of improving readability include:

a) extended line length; more space reduces the probability of truncation of long titles, but is wasteful of paper with short titles.

b) contextual wrap-around, ie bringing the end of a title to the left-hand side of a keyword and marking the end of the title with a display device, eg shading, *,/.

c) left justification, ie keywords appear on the left-hand side of the page, followed on the same line by other parts of the title.

Subarrangement at entry terms further enhances scannability. The index user is released from the necessity of scanning every entry associated with an index term and can select relevant entries by the alphabetical arrangement of qualifying terms. Both Permuterm and double KWIC indexes provide a solution.

The Permuterm index (as used in *Science and Social Sciences Citation Indexes*) is based on pairs of significant words extracted from the title. All pairs of significant terms in a title are used as the basis of index entries; such pairs are arranged alphabetically with respect to each other. An accession number accompanies each pair but no title. Accession numbers, titles and other information are printed in a separate listing.

A double KWIC index also gives subarrangement at entry terms, but is fuller than a Permuterm index in that the title is

displayed as part of the entries in the index. The first significant keyword is extracted from the title, and treated as the
main index term. This term's position in the title is then
occupied by an asterisk and the remaining words in the title
are rotated to permit each remaining significant keyword to
be displayed, using a wrap-around format, under the main
term. A similar procedure for all significant words in the title
generates a series of main terms with sub-arrangements, for
each title. Index entries are arranged alphabetically by main
term and, within a main term, alphabetically by sub-term.

KWIC-type rotation mechanisms can be applied to assigned
index terms and not merely to titles. Other rotation mechanisms will be introduced later in this section. These can also
be applied to terms in titles.

More refined computer-indexing packages instil a degree
of control into the selection of index terms. By widening
the indexing field, terms from free or controlled vocab-
ularies may be added to the title and treated in the same way
as terms in the title. Alternatively, specific terms in the
remainder of the record, in, say, the abstract, may be marked
by the indexer to be used as terms to augment the index
terms in the title. Further control may be exercised in such a
way that all of the keywords under which index entries are to
be found can be designated manually, prior to input. Exerting
this amount of control tends to undermine most of the
advantages of title indexing, but does provide for terms being
assigned in accordance with the document being indexed and
its content, rather than arbitrarily assigning a term as an index
term merely because it appears in a record. Also, with control,
terms may be signalled as comprising more than one word,
eg international economics, since two words can be signalled
as being linked.

A vocabulary may be controlled (ie only specified terms
included) although its use is not controlled (ie terms are
assigned as keywords wherever they might appear). A machine-held comparison thesaurus or go-list is a list of keywords
acceptable for computer indexing. Titles and abstracts are
matched against both the stop-list and the go-list. The presence of a term in both the input and the go-list causes an
index entry to be generated. For a fuller explanation of this
mechanism see the section on ASSASSIN in chapter seven.
This controlled procedure should lead to a good quality index.

The editing of input to KWIC programs can also contribute to the control of subject scatter. Trivial words can be suppressed, inconsistent spellings and abbreviations, word variants and multiple-word terms can be handled at the input stage, by being modified or marked by a human indexer. Cross references, input as a separate process may also alleviate subject scatter.

Indexes based on string manipulation

Controlled indexing languages (such as may be recorded in thesauri and lists of subject headings) are still preferred by many index producers including, for example, *Index medicus, Science abstracts, Engineering index,* and the *British national bibliography.* A well prepared humanly-assigned index can be based on subject content evaluation, and should therefore be easier for the searcher to use. Nevertheless, the computer still has a role in the production of indexes based on humanly-assigned index terms. The computer may be entrusted with the printing and formatting of such indexes, and is particularly useful in cumulating indexes. In addition, the computer has a hand in the generation of indexes based on string manipulation. Here, the human indexer selects a string of index terms from which the computer, under appropriate instructions, prints a series of entries for the document to which the string of index terms relate.

Articulated subject indexes

In an articulated subject index, the entry consists of a subject heading and a modifying phrase; these can be combined to form a title-like phrase. Modifying phrases are arranged alphabetically under a subject heading. The words or strings of words may be machine selected or drawn manually from a controlled vocabulary. In indexing, the words or phrases which are to appear as lead terms are indicated by the indexer. For example, the following string would cause the programs used by *World textile abstracts* to generate the type of entries given:

Indexing string

≪Soil-resistant<finishing≫of<carpets>and<wall-coverings>.

Index entries
1 Finishing
     soil-resistant, of carpets and wall-coverings.
2 Wall-coverings
     soil-resistant finishing of
3 Carpets
     soil-resistant finishing of
4 Soil-resistant, Finishing
     of carpets and wall-coverings.
The structure of the phrases is analysed, and various con-
nectives and prepositions cause the generation of different
arrays of entries. Note that prepositions are retained in the
index.

PRECIS and Current technology index (CTI)
PRECIS and CTI are rotated, or shunted, subject indexes,
based on a more rigid framework of conceptual analysis than
articulated subject indexing. A series of terms from a controlled vocabulary of simple concept terms are chosen to
represent a document. These terms are amalgamated into an
index string which also includes delimiters which denote the
way in which each term is to be treated in index entries, eg
whether it is to appear as a lead term.
   PRECIS differs from CTI indexing in its function but not
in its basic conception. *Current technology index* is a one-
stage index which contains subject headings, supplemented
by bibliographic references and 'see' and 'see also' references
in one sequence. The indexer constructs an index string
which comprises a series of index terms descriptive of the
document, separated by punctuation, which defines the
relationship between one term and its neighbour. In essence
the punctuation replaces prepositions; and the strings, read
backwards with suitable prepositions inserted, generally
constitute a sensible phrase. Terms are arranged in order of
decreasing concreteness. An example of an indexing string
and its associated entries is given below. The document to be
indexed is on 'The deep dredging of coastal estuaries'.

Indexing string
Estuaries; Coastal: Dredging, Deep

Index entries and references
1 Deep dredging: Coastal Estuaries
        see Estuaries; Coastal: Dredging, Deep
2 Dredging, Deep: Coastal Estuaries
        see Estuaries; Coastal: Dredging, Deep
3 Coastal Estuaries
        see Estuaries; Coastal
4 Estuaries; Coastal: Dredging, Deep
        Full bibliographic reference.

PRECIS is a similar set of working procedures; its main use is in the indexes to the *British national bibliography* where it is used as a subject index to a classified catalogue, but the principles are well suited to other environments. PRECIS index strings are built from a series of index terms (from a controlled vocabulary), linked together into a string by role operators. These role operators define the role of the concept represented by the term to which they are applied in the index string. Figure 9.3 shows some of the common role operators. Role operators are often represented in a 'string in brackets. The role operators are used to order concepts in the string. The main numerical operators are arranged in numerical order. To illustrate this approach with an example, the index-ing string and the index entries for a work on 'The use of boats in fly fishing for trout in still waters', are shown below:

Indexing string
(0) Still waters (1) Trout (2) Fly fishing (3) Boats.

Index entries
1 Still waters
        Trout   Fly fishing   Boats
2 Trout   Still waters
        Fly fishing   Boats
3 Fly fishing   Trout   Still waters
        Boats
4 Boats   Fly fishing   Trout   Still waters
Note: This example has been coded with role operators rela-tively simply. The use of differencing operators would have permitted more entries to be generated, and allowed, for instance, words such as 'Fishing' to take the lead position. Nevertheless this coding demonstrates the basic principles of PRECIS indexing.

CODES IN PRECIS STRINGS

Primary codes

Theme interlinks
$x	1st concept in coordinate theme
$y	2nd/subsequent concept in theme
$z	Common concept

Term codes †
$a	Common noun
$c	Proper name (class-of-one)
$d	Place name

Secondary codes

Differences

Preceding differences (3 characters)

1st and 2nd characters:
$0	Non-lead, space generating
$1	Non-lead, close-up
$2	Lead, space generating
$3	Lead, close-up

3rd character = number in the range 1 to 9 indicating level of difference

Date as a difference	$d
Parenthetical differences	
$n	Non-lead parenthetical difference
$o	Lead parenthetical difference
Connectives	
$v	Downward-reading connectives
$w	Upward-reading connective

Typographic codes †
$e	Non-filing part preceded by comma
$f	Filing part in italic preceded by comma
$g	Filing part in roman, no preceding punctuation
$h	Filing part in italic preceded by full point
$i	Filing part in italic, no preceding punctuation

† These codes are also used in the thesaurus

SCHEMA OF OPERATORS

Primary operators

Environment of core concepts	0	Location
Core concepts	1	Key system
		Thing when action not present. Thing towards which an action is directed e.g. object of transitive action, performer of intransitive action.
	2	Action; Effect of action
	3	Performer of transitive action *(agent, instrument)*; Intake; Factor
Extra-core concepts	4	Viewpoint-as-form; Aspect
	5	Selected instance, *e.g. study region, sample population*
	6	Form of document; Target user

Secondary operators

Coordinate concepts	f	'Bound' coordinate concept
	g	Standard coordinate concept
Dependent elements	p	Part; Property
	q	Member of quasi-generic group
	r	Assembly
Special classes of action	s	Role definer; Directional property
	t	Author-attributed association
	u	Two-way interaction

Note on prefixes to Codes. The codes in the left-hand panel are marked as instructions, as opposed to data, by their preceding symbols. These are shown as dollar signs ($) to reflect current practice in many PRECIS files, but any non-alpha-numeric character will serve the same purpose. The draft version of the *UNIMARC Manual* (referring to PRECIS data in Field 670) states that "signs used as subfield codes (in UNIMARC, the $) *should be avoided*".

Figure 9.3: PRECIS operators and codes

There are three positions in an index entry:

Lead   Qualifier
       Display

and the terms are shunted through these positions to create the series of index entries. Note that each entry shows the lead term in context and is in effect a PRECIS of the subject of the document.

In both PRECIS and CTI, 'see' and 'see also' references between individual terms and related terms can be input as a distinct operation. If such relationships are noted on the first use of an index term, then thereafter the presence of that term will trigger the printing of appropriate references. For example:

Prejudice see also Sexism
Press see also Journalism
Philately see Postage stamps.

Other indexes

There are various other rotational indexing systems. We will demonstrate three of these by using A, B and C to represent three indexing terms. Selective Listing in Combination (SLIC) indexing involves the combination of elements in one direction only. In other words the index entries from an index string ABC would be ABC, AC, BC, and C. Cyclic indexing is based on the shunting of the lead term into the last position until each element has occupied the lead position. The entries would be: ABC, BCA, CAB. Rotated indexing is achieved by retaining the same citation order, but underlining the elements acting as the lead term. For example: $\underline{A}$BC, A$\underline{B}$C, AB$\underline{C}$.

The computer-generated version of a post-coordinate index is the dual dictionary. Not unlike a simple subject index, accession numbers are listed under index terms. The dictionary is intended to be used by comparing the numbers listed beneath two or more headings. Usually two (hence dual) or more copies of the dictionary are compared side-by-side, and thus documents for which combinations of separate terms have been assigned can be identified.

Citation indexing is a means of producing an effective index by exploiting the computer's capacity for arranging and re-formatting entries. Input to the indexing system comprises the references of recent articles in relatively few core journals and, for each article, the list of works that it refers to. A citation index then lists 'cited' documents together with a list of those items that have cited them (citing articles). This is an effective way of covering a fairly wide subject field with almost no human intervention. The prime examples of citation indexes are those produced by the Institute for Scientific Information, ie *Social sciences, Arts and humanities* and *Science citation indexes.* Thus, given one document in a field, the searcher should be able to trace other related documents. However, the many inconsistencies in citation standards cause problems, and the reasons for citing a document are not always to do with shared subject content. More details on the products of the Institute for Scientific Information are to be found in chapter five.

Further reading

Armitage, J E and Lynch, M F 'Some structural characteristics of articulated subject indexes'. *Information storage and retrieval* 4 1968. 101-11.

Austin, D 'The development of PRECIS: a theoretical and technical history'. *Journal of documentation* 30(2) 1974. 47-102.

Austin, D *PRECIS: a manual of concept analysis and subject indexing.* 2nd ed. London, BLBSD, 1984.

Austin, D and Digger, J A 'PRECIS: the PREserved Context Index System'. *Library resources and technical services* 21(1) Winter 1977. 13-30.

Feinberg, H (ed) Indexing specialised formats and subjects Metuchen (N J); London, Scarecrow Press, 1983.

Feinburg, H *Title derivative indexing techniques: a comparative study.* Los Angeles, Scarecrow Press, 1975.

Foskett, A C *The subject approach to information.* 4th ed. London, Bingley, 1982.

Hunter, E J and Bakewell, K G B *Cataloguing.* 2nd rev. and expanded ed. London, Bingley, 1983. (Outlines of modern librarianship).

Langridge, D 'Review of PRECIS'. *Journal of librarianship* 8(3) 1976. 210-12.

Matthews, F W and Shillingford, A D 'Variations on KWIC'. *Aslib proceedings* 25(4) 1973. 140-52.

Ramsden, M J *PRECIS: a workbook for students of librarianship.* London, Bingley, 1981.

Rowley, J E 'Printed versus online indexes'. *The indexer* 13(3)
    April 1983. 188-9.
Thomas, P A 'The use of KWIC to index the proceedings of a
    public enquiry'. *The indexer* 8(3) April 1973. 145-52.

Chapter Ten

Library housekeeping operations and the computer

Computers are widely exploited in library housekeeping operations. These are the activities which permit libraries to keep a record of their stock, and the whereabouts and status of the stock. The three chapters that follow divide library housekeeping operations into three groups: acquisitions, ordering and cataloguing systems; circulation control and document-delivery systems; and finally serials control systems. Virtually all larger public library authorities and most large university, polytechnic and college libraries have computerized housekeeping systems, or make use of the products of such systems. The impact of the system will vary from one library to another, as will the extent of computerization. Equally, some systems incorporate all of the newest options, whereas other libraries are operating systems which they still find to be perfectly satisfactory, but which do not incorporate all of the latest technology and software.

Computerized housekeeping systems, have, despite the prevalence of information-retrieval systems in special libraries, been less common amongst special libraries, than in their larger counterparts in the public and academic library sectors. Nevertheless, the larger special libraries which have been concerned to process large numbers of transactions now have extensive experience of computerized systems. The introduction of microcomputers and associated software has significantly enhanced the possibilities for the use of computerized housekeeping systems in smaller libraries. There has been a growth in the extent of the use of computerized cataloguing and circulation control systems in the past two to three years.

The nature of the application of computers varies between the sectors. In cataloguing, public libraries may benefit to a greater extent than, say, university libraries, from centrally or cooperatively created catalogue records. The relatively small number of service points in many academic libraries make them easier targets for the computerization of circulation routines (since less equipment need be installed) than public libraries.

The reasons for opting for a computerized housekeeping system are many and various. Several of the factors outlined in chapter one can be expected to apply. Computers permit the reduction of the number of repetitive tasks. In general, data will only be input once, and thereafter can be accessed and amended. Computer-based systems may be cheaper or more efficient. They may lead to the introduction of services not previously available, such as the automatic control of overborrowing and the trapping of reserved books on their return to the library. An important asset of a computer-based system is the added control over all library functions that can be achieved with the aid of more comprehensive library-management statistics. Such statistics make it easier to justify a good cause, and facilitate the evaluation of various courses of action.

All library housekeeping routines are directed towards controlling the stock of a library. Such routines may include selection, ordering, acquisitions, labelling, cataloguing and circulation control. In many functions the computer acts primarily as an information source on the state of the stock, and hence must hold records which describe the stock and its whereabouts. This information may be available online or via printed lists, in order to investigate, for example, 'what is in stock?' or 'what is on loan to whom?' Occasionally, the computer-based system may actually control the stock; for example, by using a trapping store, which triggers a light or a 'buzz' when a reserved book is returned to the circulation desk. The more up-to-date the information in the computer files, the better is the control of the housekeeping operation. In some applications such as ordering and cataloguing, it is less essential than in others to have the very latest information on the state of a particular transaction. Most systems are designed to cover the majority of the book and non-book material stock of a library. Serials, however, because of their ongoing nature, pose special problems, especially in the area of acquisition and subscription control.

Many library housekeeping systems have been developed

for, and with the participation of, the library using the system and thus there is a wide variety of different systems. Nevertheless, within this environment, there is still an awareness of the economies to be gained by cooperative efforts. Computers have to be seen as a means towards sharing bibliographic data, and, to some extent, library stock, whilst retaining the ability to provide a specialist service to the library's own membership.

The automation of housekeeping routines may be piecemeal or integrated, or planned in instalments which contribute towards an integrated final system. Often there is a chain reaction. A library may start with a circulation system but, to enhance this, the library needs machine-readable book records in order to produce meaningful overdue notices and therefore turns to a computerized stock record or catalogue. A catalogue shows what is available in the library. This cataloguing system may be enhanced by an ordering and acquisitions subsystem which indicates what will be available, and is thus important for the latest and most recent items. The development and implementation of subsystems may not follow this route; cataloguing subsystems may precede circulation control subsystems, for example.

The piecemeal approach is commonly adopted, because it is not always clear initially that computerization will be profitable for more than one application. Piecemeal implementation is also easier and has the advantage of concentrating effort on the most urgent areas. The unnecessary mechanization of satisfactory manual systems is avoided. The main drawback of piecemeal implementation, is the likelihood of future incompatibility. In particular, it is important to select a cooperative or a software package which has other subsystems available as part of the complete system, or with which the system currently being considered is compatible. It may not always be desirable or feasible to opt for complete integration in the computerization of library housekeeping, but it is always desirable to have options and subsystems available so that they can be purchased in the future, as funds become available, and as the need for such systems develops. Some of the earlier libraries to experiment with computerization can be forgiven for the piecemeal approach that they were obliged to adopt. However, the piecemeal approach has not uncommonly led to a library having different software packages, from different software suppliers, operating on different types of computers for each of that library's major housekeeping functions. This obviously leaves plenty of scope for duplication of effort and general muddle.

An integrated system is one where the files are interlinked so that deletions, additions and other changes in one file automatically activate appropriate changes in related files. Integrated systems are becoming increasingly popular as libraries computerize more than one subsystem and become more confident of the success of computerization projects. Certainly most of the cooperatives and others involved in developing systems in this field are moving towards offering integrated systems, even if some of the subsystems for some operators are closer to figments of the imagination than to being operational systems. Integrated systems frequently link order and acquisitions systems with cataloguing systems, or cataloguing systems with circulation systems, or interlink all three stages. An integrated system overcomes any qualms about compatibility, offers greater scope for staff saving and better provision of management information.

Cooperatives and other options
Many very significant developments in computerized library housekeeping systems have been achieved or initiated by cooperative ventures, with a number of independent libraries working together towards some common benefit. Many of the more important cooperatives are featured in the next few chapters, and include OCLC, BLCMP, SWALCAP, LASER, UTLAS to name but a few. Many of these cooperatives were formed originally in order to facilitate resource sharing, and to make it possible for the materials available in one library to be accessed by the users of another library. A central feature of any resource-sharing venture is a record which shows the holdings of the cooperative libraries. This record will normally take the form of a union catalogue which shows details of the holdings of all participating libraries. Obviously if the holdings of the participating libraries are significant these union catalogues can be significant bibliographic tools. Prior to computerized housekeeping, the creation of such a union catalogue was a tedious and too often expensive operation. Card-form union catalogues required that the cards holding the records of all the participating libraries' stocks be

collated and interfiled. The keeping of more than one copy of such a catalogue involved producing more copies of cards and filing these into a further sequence. Computerization permitted the maintenance of union catalogues and also facilitated the compilation of the catalogues of the participating libraries. A number of cooperatives then developed systems for creating union catalogues, some developing their own software, and others adopting and modifying software that was available elsewhere. Nevertheless, the desire to share resources, and thus enhance services to users, has been responsible for the initiation of many housekeeping systems. On the other hand, it is important to remember that true resource sharing has not yet been achieved. Current developments in document-delivery systems promise to speed up access to the documents available in libraries other than the one to which a user submits his request.

Thus, when a library comes to consider computerization, one option is to become a member of a cooperative and to take advantage of the systems being offered and developed by the cooperative. Another option is to participate in a national group, such as, in the United Kingdom, the BLAISE LOCAS network. This is in some ways similar to a cooperative in that there is the opportunity to share resources and expertise which is central to the operation of a cooperative, but could in broad terms be said to differ from a cooperative in that there is more evident leadership. The group is led by its instigators, who⁻ might be the national library. The final option when a library is making a choice of a computerized housekeeping system is to purchase a commercially available turnkey system, such as that available from GEAC Computers Ltd.

Basically cooperatives have a history of influence in computerized library housekeeping systems. In the future, other options may threaten their continued existence. Some of the commercial vendors of software packages are able to offer more sophisticated software. Two factors are likely to assure the continuation of cooperatives in some form:

a) the shared database which is a feature of the processing which leads to the union catalogue, and which holds the union catalogue records.

b) shared expertise, which is very important for moral support. The cooperative offers a framework for a forum in which a variety of difficulties can be shared and sometimes resolved.

Example — University of York
The library of the University of York began computerized housekeeping operations with a circulation-control system. This led to the creation of a master bookfile, which was updated daily by online catalogue record amendment, initially producing catalogue cards. Before greater use could be made of this master bookfile considerable effort had to be directed towards perfecting the bookfile, in order that it was simple, clean and visually pleasant to use. The file had to be checked by professional staff, edited and amended as necessary, before it could be used in some of the other applications below: The development of the University's system is a good example of the movement towards integrated housekeeping operations.

1 Online enquiry system enhancements mean that it is possible to use author's name or headings, or a reader's surname to access information in the master file. The VDU will display author/heading, title and classmark of all relevant items in the bookfile of 300,000 entries. Four entries can then be selected, and more complete bibliographical entries can be viewed for those four. In addition, for each of the four records the name and address of the borrower (if on loan), the loan and due dates and whether any notices have been sent to the reader will be shown. This information is available to staff, and the same information, with the exception of the borrower information, is available to the public, at over sixty terminals on campus and off campus. It is also possible to key in the first ten characters of the reader's surname and the library's screen will show details of his status and address within the university, all loans, due dates and any notices received. Borrowers can view this data for their own loans only.

2 The periodicals catalogue is a subsystem of the main bibliographic database. Each entry consists of the Plessey (now DS Ltd) base number, heading, title, date and classmark information, with additional classmarks for multi-discipline journals. In addition there is information on publisher, frequency, agent and holdings. This information can be sorted and printed on classmark, agent, publisher, frequency or any combination of these. Updating is online and information is accessible via interactive terminals. Updated periodicals catalogues are produced at regular intervals on microfiche or paper.

3   Atkinson Store: A record of items which are taken from the main stock for possible eventual disposal is kept by allocating a pseudo-borrower number, and the location is amended in the catalogues.

4   Stocktaking: A stocktaking exercise in 1982 was facilitated by the computerized circulation system. A Plessey portable data-capture unit was used. Book numbers were read on shelves and the data of the books present transmitted to the mainframe. Each day a print-out of the preceding day's work was received. Books which had been mis-shelved, or returned to the shelves undischarged, and other problems could be identified. These books were then sorted, and at the completion of a section, the computer produced lists for those book numbers for which no match had been found.

5   Title catalogue: This is a simple quick-reference catalogue containing brief entries arranged according to title. The first edition was produced on microfiche, but this will eventually be a feature of the online enquiry facility.

6   Classified catalogue and subject index: It is the intention to make the classified catalogue available both on microfiche and online, and the subject index on paper print-out as well as online, over the next few years.

Chapter Eleven

Acquisitions, ordering and cataloguing systems

Many cataloguing and acquisitions systems are integrated, and the two processes interact, since cataloguing follows acquisition. This chapter will treat acquisition and ordering systems as distinct subsystems from cataloguing subsystems, but both are grouped here in order that some of the cases described at the end of the chapter can be used to illustrate the integrated approach.

Ordering and acquisitions systems
Many ordering and acquisitions systems are now computer-based. The ordering process is particularly suited to computer-ization, as it is a relatively simple clerical process, where similar operations are applicable to all categories of library. Most ordering systems concentrate on monographs and other once-and-for-all purchases. In keeping with normal practice this section will concentrate on these materials and leave serials acquisition to chapter thirteen.

The functions of an ordering or acquisitions system can be specified basically as:

 a)   To receive records of items to be acquired;

 b)   To establish whether items requested are already in stock or on order;

 c)   To print orders or otherwise order items;

 d) To check when orders are overdue and follow up overdue orders;

 e)   To maintain a file of records of items on order;

 f)   To note the arrival of ordered items and prepare for payment;

 g)   To maintain book-fund statistics and accounts.

Some libraries also like an ordering system to notify individ-uals of the receipt of items, and produce various listings of books on order or recently acquired.

Input to an ordering system which is to satisfy the above functions must include: a) details of new orders; b) amendments or corrections to existing orders; c) booksellers' reports; and d) details of received books. All requests for an order must be checked, to ensure that the item is not already in stock or on order and to guarantee that the bibliographic record of the item is accurate. Some of this checking can be performed by matching of items requested against computer files of existing stock or other bibliographic records. This is only likely to be successful, where the citation given by the requester is at least partially accurate; ISBNs are particularly important in this respect. With the aid of the computer, bibliographic records for new orders may be drawn either from a file of MARC records, from a file of existing items in the library, from a file of cooperative records, or from local inputting. Order records of each item typically include: book number (eg ISBN), short bibliographic details, number of copies ordered, estimated price, currency, bookseller, book fund. Such bibliographic records comprise the main file of current orders. A second file must contain names and addresses of booksellers used by the library and this file must also be open to alterations. The order file must be amended as books arrive, or as booksellers notify non-availability, etc.

The process is initiated by adding orders to the order file; this prompts the dispatch of orders to the supplier. When the item is received the order records become the basis of catalogue records. In an integrated ordering and cataloguing system, order records may be examined on a VDU and upgraded to cataloguing standards. Alternatively, a batch of print-out or printed slips may be passed to the cataloguing section. At this stage, book cards may also be generated for use in the circulation system. At regular intervals the computer checks for the orders that remain unfulfilled. In summary then, the outputs from an ordering system are typically:

printed listings of the order file
an accessions register (of recent items acquired)
accounts
chasers
recommendations for future acquisitions
statistics
book cards
processing slips.

In ordering systems, batch-processed operations are generally satisfactory. The initiative for online operation of ordering systems generally develops within an integrated online system. It is quite satisfactory to add to the order file in batches and to check the progress of orders and finances at intervals, provided the gaps between the processing of adjacent batches is reasonably short. It is less important than in, say, a circulation control system, to be able to trace a specific record, since interactions with the library's public are rare. However, online operation, or at least online inputting, is reckoned to reduce the probability of errors in orders.

Cataloguing systems

The past ten years have witnessed a revolution in cataloguing practice. Cataloguing standards have been rationalized and more widely acknowledged and new physical forms of catalogue have made their debut. The impact of computers during these ten years has been significant.

The catalogue has always been regarded by librarians as an important tool. Computerization has reinforced this situation, since the catalogue, the primary record of the stock of a library, can now be utilized in many more contexts. Soon, nearly all libraries will use the computer in the generation of catalogues. Public libraries are well accustomed to mechanized catalogues. Some London boroughs saw computerization as a means of merging different physical forms of catalogues, classification schemes, filing orders and cataloguing rules, as early as 1964. Barnet, Camden and Greenwich were early in adopting a computer-based solution. Other United Kingdom public libraries followed suit in 1974 and 1975, when they too were faced with local authority re-organization. Public libraries benefit especially from shared catalogue records, and may use records created by central agencies or other libraries. Since it is common for items in public libraries to be in more than one library's collection somebody else's catalogue records may be very useful. Academic libraries tend to have more unique stocks which include special collections, and thus do not profit so extensively from cooperative ventures. Nevertheless, academic libraries are implementing computerized cataloguing systems.

Many special libraries have also inaugurated a computerized system but, since catalogue records are usually less numerous in this environment, cataloguing systems in special libraries are likely to be integrated into a total information system. Many of the software packages which offer text retrieval are equally capable of maintaining a catalogue-record database, as they are of recording other types of bibliographic records. Some software packages have special cataloguing subsystems which facilitate the formatting or printing of catalogue records. Special libraries by their very nature tend to have unique collections, and therefore do not necessarily benefit from participation in cooperatives, etc. Although some are members of groups like BLAISE LOCAS, in general the type of cataloguing system encountered in special libraries is not likely to be one of those which is well known in larger academic and public libraries. Hence, there is plenty of experience in the computerization of cataloguing systems and a wide variety of different solutions. Some libraries have implemented home-grown systems, others participate in national, regional or *ad hoc* cooperative schemes, and others exploit packages and turnkey systems.

Mechanization offers a welcome opportunity to re-assess objectives. What is a catalogue and to what uses can it be put? A catalogue is an organized record of the stock of a library or a library system. Union catalogues are catalogues generated centrally or cooperatively, reflecting the stock of more than one library or library system. Catalogues are distinct from indexes in that their preoccupation is with complete documents and they tend to give a full bibliographic description of the documents described. But, in many senses, a catalogue is merely a file of bibliographic records, little different from any other database used in information retrieval. Catalogues can be organized in two different ways, giving rise to dictionary or classified catalogues. The dictionary catalogue, more common in the United States, contains bibliographic records entered under author, title and alphabetical subject headings, integrated into one sequence. The classified catalogue, almost universal in the United Kingdom, comprises at least three separate sequences: a name catalogue or an author/title catalogue, a classified subject catalogue and a subject index to the classified catalogue. Catalogues may also vary in the amount of detail that is given in each bibliographic record and in the extent of references and added entries.

The structure and format of a catalogue should be chosen

with an eye to its function. All catalogues give access to a library collection via a number of access points. In this context, some catalogues are basically finding tools. The average library patron uses the catalogue as a finding list, as an aid to discovering whether a library has a book, and if it has, where that book is shelved. Other catalogues perform as bibliographical tools and hence must be more detailed and refined; any edition of a book must be differentiated from others, for purposes of selection, acquisition and study. National libraries are under some obligation to adhere to the standards required of a bibliographical tool, since they are responsible for national bibliographic control, and hence the records that they generate may not always be suitable for local library use. The functions of the catalogue need to be evaluated in terms of the demands of the users and those of the librarian. Catalogues are used extensively for bibliographic checking, stock editing, stocktaking, readers service enquiries, reference work, lending, ordering and catalogue maintenance.

Components of a cataloguing system

The objective of any computerized cataloguing system is to create appropriate catalogues. To this end, records may be drawn from any of the following sources:

The UK or LC files of MARC records;

A union file of the stock of several libraries;

A file of records held by the library (ie the records that comprise the existing library catalogue);

Local cataloguing.

The bibliographical records contained within these files may be selected manually or with the intercession of a computer. Acceptable records, after modification to match local requirements (eg indication of added entries, references) and the addition of local data (eg class numbers, location) are added to the main or master file of catalogue records of the library's holdings. If batch-processing is employed, the catalogue records are added in a batch and merged into the master or a cumulative file. The cumulative file, where it exists, is a file of the recently added records. Being smaller than the total master file, the temporary cumulative file can be printed more cheaply than the total master file and thus forms the basis of addenda to the catalogue. Batch processing is satisfactory for the production of listings, such as booksellers' orders and catalogues, but the possibility of errors and the associated repeat processing, make the online creation and editing of records desirable.

When online processing is available, existing records can be inspected, and new records created at an online terminal. This option is rapidly becoming the norm.

After checking and editing, records are added to the master file; the merging of records into the master file is sometimes a batch job. Cheshire County Public Library was one of the early libraries to opt for an online system. Some libraries find it too expensive to hold all files online and make only the most active files available online. Data that is needed for ordering and cataloguing of new titles is in online files, but more static files, such as the catalogue itself, are consulted on regularly updated COM output. On a specified date, at the end of a month or quarter, the master file and the cumulative file will be sorted into the required order and the catalogue generated in the chosen physical form.

Online catalogue consultation by library staff for catalogue record amendment and updating is now common. Many systems are now developing public-access online catalogues, where the user is able to consult the catalogue at an online terminal, usually in the form of a VDU. GEAC was one of the earlier vendors to offer this facility in the United Kingdom, and using the GEAC system online public-access catalogues first became available in the United Kingdom at the University of Hull and the Polytechnic of the South Bank. In the United States various experiments have been conducted in order to investigate user response to public-access catalogues in online form. Although some progress has been made in this direction, there is scope for further investigation into the most effective design for online public-access catalogues, and this is an area in which many developments can be expected in the next few years.

There are three other physical forms of catalogue that are encountered in conjunction with a computerized cataloguing system: catalogue cards, computer book-form catalogues and COM catalogues. Catalogue cards are the conventional form and as such were favoured by libraries in the early computerization projects (eg Aston University, OCLC), since they avoided discontinuities in catalogue provision. However, as manual filing remains as a necessary evil, the catalogue is still open to mis-filing and the economies of machine filing cannot be fully exploited, this form is rapidly losing popularity.

Computer-produced book-form catalogues were also fashionable in early systems. For example, Coventry City Libraries began issuing a computer-produced book catalogue in 1969, which covered non-fiction in author and classified lists. The London Borough of Barnet started with a book-form catalogue in 1965 and Hatfield Polytechnic's computer-produced book catalogue began in 1970. Many libraries retain this form for some listings such as subject indexes (eg Aston University, Birmingham Polytechnic), catalogues of smaller specialist collections and short-entry listings (eg Wolverhampton Polytechnic). Book-form catalogues are regarded as simple to use, and can be located on any site without recourse to further machinery. Hence, book form may be chosen for catalogues to be distributed to branch public libraries.

Some of the problems, such as cost and bulk, of a line-printer catalogue can be alleviated by a typeset catalogue. Such catalogues boast high typographic quality, with upper and lower case characters and a more compact form than line print-out.

The microfilm catalogue produced by COM, is widespread. Despite some doubts regarding its agreeableness in use, the microfilm catalogue offers: compact storage; low material costs, even for multiple copies; inexpensive reproduction; ability fo cumulate frequently, since a new edition can be issued regularly eg once a month; and easy and cheap distribution by post or carrier.

All of the forms in which microfilm is available may be enlisted for catalogues. Cassetted and open roll, 35mm and 16mm, microfiche, superfiche and ultrafiche, are all possible fomats, although there is some trend towards microfiche. There are also a variety of reduction ratios (eg 24x, 42x, 48x), layouts for catalogue entries, modes of presenting pages on a fiche or film, and positive or negative film from which to choose. *Books in English* is produced on ultrafiche, with an extra high reduction ratio. For reading, microfilms must be inserted in an appropriate reader. Readers must be selected in accordance with film type. Information and advice concerning films and readers can be obtained from the National Reprographic Centre for Documentation, based at Hatfield Polytechnic.

Cataloguing systems — some examples

Within the broad outline of a mechanized cataloguing system, there is scope for great disparity between one system and the next. There are cooperative and non-cooperative schemes, integrated and less integrated options, and MARC and non-MARC systems. Some important examples and organizations are explored below.

1 *The Library of Congress* remains the centralized cataloguing agency of prime importance to American libraries. The machine-readable cataloguing records which are now generated by the LC, LC MARC, are important in both American and British libraries. The cataloguing products, which extend to proofsheets, printed catalogues, MARC tapes, and Cataloguing-in-Publication data, are merely an extension of the cataloguing activities of the LC, and thus, records are made available for items in the LC.

The current LC MARC database contains both records created by the LC staff and those created by cooperating libraries and verified by the LC. Most of the records are for post-1966 publications, but as a result of the RECON Project (retrospective conversion) and the COMARC Project (cooperative machine-readable cataloguing), records for many earlier materials are also present. The database is made available to other libraries in the form of magnetic tapes.

2 *BLAISE,* the British Library Automated Information Service, became operational in 1977. It is related to BNB in that any of the BLAISE services exploit the UKMARC database and other databases generated by the British Library Bibliographic Services Division, such as the *British Education Index.* BLAISE offers a variety of services bridging the cataloguing and information-retrieval functions.

LOCAS or the Local Catalogue Service was introduced in 1974 to offer a complete cataloguing service, from data preparation to catalogue output, for those libraries who would like to benefit from the advantages of centralized computer processing, but who do not wish to manage the computerized processing for themselves. This centralized system offers libraries an extensive range of options in terms of the frequency of catalogue production, and the physical form of catalogue. For each participating library LOCAS maintains a

MARC-based catalogue file consisting of centrally produced UK and LCMARC records, and locally created records for material which is present in the collection of that library, but for which records are not available in the BL database. Libraries may add local data, such as class numbers or location information to the records which they select to add to their file. Most LOCAS subscribers are individual libraries who have established a direct relationship with LOCAS. However, LOCAS does support some libraries acting in groups, such as the member libraries of SCOLCAP and the members of the University of London's Cooperative Scheme.

Tape services: For organizations with access to computing facilities, BLBSD offers the *Selective Record Service* and MARC *Exchange Tapes.* The *Selective Record Service* enables libraries to submit requests for individual records from the British Library databases in machine-readable form. Records are identified by their control number offline, or by a wide range of search keys online. Regular monthly outputs can be supplied, or other arrangements can be made to suit the client. The *Exchange Tape Service* enables libraries to build large bibliographic files for in-house use. Weekly tapes of current records, or cumulated back files available as separate year cumulations or at block rates, can be supplied.

Cataloguing-in-Publication (CIP) is not so much a service, but a feature of UKMARC databases. It merits a separate mention, and is therefore introduced in this context. The object of CIP is to provide advance information of forthcoming British books. The CIP data are compiled by the BLBSD from preliminary pages of forthcoming works whilst these are still in proof form. The CIP data is then published: in the book itself, in BNB, on BNB cards, and on the UKMARC tapes. Sometimes it will be necessary to upgrade CIP records once the book is published, and this process is undertaken by BLBSD as appropriate. CIP is intended to facilitate the selection and ordering of materials by alerting librarians and others to forthcoming works in advance of their publication.

Microprocessor systems BLAISE offers two packages for off-line editing on intelligent terminals. These permit editing and amendment of records offline, and thus reduce online costs, since records are only selected online. BIBDES (Bibliographic

Data Entry System) uses an ICL 150L computer and CORTEX runs on a Sirius 128K machine.

3 OCLC, the Online Computer Library Center, was founded in 1967 by a group of Ohio college libraries. In its early years it benefitted from a variety of grants to support activities and developments, but since 1971, OCLC has been supported by membership fees and grants for specific research and development projects. Now OCLC has around 3,000 members, most of them in North America, but some in other parts of the world. OCLC is based upon extensive bibliographic databases which have been and continue to be built and shared by OCLC members. Although essentially a cooperative scheme with a central database, OCLC also offers a local processing option. The two options then are:

a) Centralized option: Libraries may have direct access to the files held on a computer in Ohio. The central file is the Online Union Catalogue, which contains almost 10 million bibliographic records, from all members. About one third of the new records are contributed by LC, the National Library of Medicine, the National Agricultural Library and the United States Government Printing Office. This union catalogue contains MARC records for monographs, serials, audio-visual, maps, manuscripts, sound recordings and scores. Records may be searched on ISBN and other standard numbers, and also on search keys derived from names and titles.

In cataloguing wherever possible records from the Online Union Catalogue are utilized. If original cataloguing is necessary the LC name authority file is available to help in establishing headings. New records are available to other OCLC users as soon as they are entered. Catalogue output is available as COM, cards, magnetic tape and accessions lists.

The acquisitions system integrates data from the online Union Catalogue with local order and fund data, thus improving order processing and providing current accounting information. The OCLC database is searched for the appropriate record, and if this is present it may be used in initiating the order. If this is not available, a record can be created on a form online. The receipt of materials and invoices and suppliers' reports are recorded in acquisitions records. The acquisitions system uses a name-address directory as its source of address information for orders.

The serials control system handles check-in, claiming and union listing of serial publications. There is online access to current, detailed copy-specific holdings and location information in the individual library and from union list groups. The CONSER (conversion of serials) project built up a large serials database.

The interlibrary loan system increases resource sharing by providing effective loan processing. This system is used both in the United States and between the United Kingdom and European countries and the United States. The intending borrower merely specifies a search key for the item he wishes to borrow, and the system provides a bibliographic description, and permits the requester to specify up to five potential lending libraries, and the system transmits the requests to these libraries one at a time.

b) Local Library System LS/2000: OCLC is developing a local library system, that will eventually include circulation control and online catalogues. The local system is designed to be flexible enough to meet the needs of a single library or those of a library cluster. OCLC's local system will permit libraries to automate in stages. Eventually the LS/2000 will support circulation and cataloguing and provide online public-access catalogues, administrative control, and serials check-in. The library can define its own authority files, indexes, bibliographic and patron-record contents and other features. It is thus possible to design a local system tailored to the needs of the individual library within the range of options available with LS/2000.

OCLC Europe supports a nationwide telecommunications network in the United Kingdom and Ireland to provide users with dedicated access to the OCLC databases and associated services in the US. The OCLC Europe network is connected to the OCLC computer system in the US by a dedicated link via an undersea cable.

4 LASER, the London and South-Eastern Region, is an organization for library cooperation within Greater London, and various counties in the south-east of England. LASER operates an interlending service which is based upon its union catalogue. A transport scheme is operated for interlending in London and the south-east, and various bibliographic services are offered based on LASER's minicomputer.

There are currently 1.23 million records on the LASER minicomputer system, representing the 40 million volumes held in member libraries. The LASER minicomputer system is in union catalogue form, and includes UKMARC records as well as LCMARC records for books acquired by LASER libraries, and records generated by LASER member libraries. Records can be accessed by author, title and book number. A microfiche version of the LASER database, the LASER union catalogue on microfiche, shows records to the end of 1982 in author order. A selective record service and a card service is available to member libraries for records relating to their collections.

5 *BLCMP* (originally Birmingham Libraries Cooperative Mechanization Project) is a cooperative venture which embraces both network and stand-alone services, and batch and online services. Formed in 1969, the first operational system was implemented in 1972/3. Today, BLCMP offers services to nearly 50 member libraries, including public libraries, university libraries, polytechnic libraries and others. The shared systems are run on an IBM 4341 computer housed at BLCMP. The shared online system 'BOSS' utilizes a private telecommunications network.

BLCMP maintains extensive databases of MARC records. All UKMARC data is available, LCMARC from 1972 and BLCMP member libraries Extra-MARC cataloguing. The database contains a large number of audio-visual items, music and serials. Online interactive searching can be performed on author/title acronyms and traditional control-number searching is possible and the only means of access on the offline batch system.

The cataloguing systems were the first to be developed. The first systems were batch mode and batch-mode catalogue-record processing is still available. BOSS (BLCMP Online Support Service) provides a fully integrated online acquisitions and cataloguing system. The online cataloguing system allows users to search for, edit and create records. Tailored formats are provided on the screen for the input and amendment of records. Records are of two types: general bibliographic records which contain the basic bibliographic data, and local records relating to local information of particular interest to an individual library. An extensive name authority file is maintained. BLCMP produces union and individual library catalogues, and these last are available in a range of formats. The union catalogues are on microfiche. An online public-access facility is being developed.

The acquisitions and ordering system provides facilities for the ordering and receipt of library materials. Records of items on order or recently received are created, consulted and amended online. The acquisitions system is presently only available to subscribers to BOSS, but will be offered as a stand-alone option at a later date. Prior to creation of an order record, the user may search to discover whether an item is already in stock, and to ascertain its bibliographic details. BLCMP databases include CIP data and will be enhanced to cover data from suppliers' databases. Any record may be used for inclusion in an order, and tailored input formats facilitate the creation of orders. Various other facilities are available such as printed orders, chasing, and maintenance of records. The order can be retrieved for receipt details to be added when the document arrives.

BLCMP's circulation control system, CIRCO, can be extensively tailored to meet local requirements. CIRCO oper-ates as a stand-alone circulation package but may also be linked to BLCMP's centralized cataloguing and acquisitions services. BLCMP's stand-alone systems run on Data General Eclipse computers, a range covering both micros and main-frames. CIRCO incorporates all of the usual functions associated with the issue, return and reservation of library materials. Data-capture units are light pens, and such units can be made available at various locations in the library for public consultation. Enquiries can be made to discover the status of particular records. Access is available by author/title key and classmark, as well as by control number and charging number. Online public access catalogues are under further development.

Other facilities include the possibility of generating: current accessions lists, subject indexes, selected sequences, regional library bureaux notifications and printed accessions registers.

6 *SWALCAP* is a non-profit-making organization based at the University of Bristol. Established in 1969, SWALCAP has been financially self-sufficient since 1979. The aim of SWALCAP is to provide integrated computer services for library housekeeping purposes, and to keep these services

up-to-date. Its primary function is to provide a centre for software and hardware expertise for its members, and in order to achieve this it has its own computer centre.

SWALCAP supports a network arrangement of remote terminals and minicomputers linked to the central computer via private lines. All online facilities are available from all terminals. Access to individual transactions is made via a menu which lists each application as detailed: circulation, direct data entry, print files, terminal system control, cataloguing.

The Mk II circulation system is an enhanced version of a system which was originally the core of the SWALCAP services. The service centres on an online short-title catalogue and on online registration file. For libraries with catalogue records in MARC format the short-title catalogue can be created automatically from this database. Some terminals will be linked to telepens for issue, return and renew functions. Enquiries as to the status of items may be input through any terminal. Management information is available for loan statistics.

The cataloguing service has been in use since 1978. From 1984 a Mk II cataloguing and acquisitions system has been in operation. In this Mk II system all records in the database will be available online and are accessible by control number, author/title, or title and author acronym keys. A link between the MARC records in the catalogue system and the circulation system permits the records in the short-title catalogue to be displayed in full. Online editing and amendment of catalogue records and a variety of modes of output is available for the nineteen member libraries.

6 *UKLDS* is more of a database and a set of software for the support of a database, than a cataloguing cooperative. Nevertheless, in the sense that the UKLDS is a cooperative cataloguing venture it has a place in this section. The UKLDS or the UK Library Database System is a proposal from the Cooperative Automation Group (CAG) which was first disseminated in a discussion paper published in 1982. CAG's membership consists basically of representatives from each of the British Library cooperatives, BLCMP, LASER, SCOLCAP, SWALCAP, and from BLBSD, and Aslib, the LA, SCONUL and COPOL. Initially, the proposal was for the establishment

of a centralized database, and the software to support the establishment and communication with the database, which will support shared cataloguing requirements. This database would ·have allowed the cooperatives to pool all extra-MARC records created by the members of the cooperatives, and would thus eventually become a very substantial bibliographic database. A proposed input standard for records in the UKLDS for monographs was published in 1983. This standard is compatible with AACR2 and the UKMARC format. Input standards for various other media and arrangements for subject access were considered. In mid-1984, the CAG concluded that it was not realistic to pursue the establishment of a UKLDS in the way originally conceived, but instead envisaged a loose series of working arrangements resulting in the exchange of data between different parties on mutually agreed terms.

7 *Other cooperatives:* There are many other networks which support cataloguing activities, and most of them are exploiting computerized systems.

SCOLCAP is based on the National Library of Scotland, and has around twenty member libraries. An integrated online cataloguing and acquisitions system is in the process of being developed. Local cooperatives, such as NEMROC (Newcastle Media Resources Organization Committee) and SHEMROC, a similar group for the Sheffield area, also support cataloguing activities.

In the United States there are also a number of local networks which support cataloguing and other activities. WLN (Washington Library Network) is composed of libraries in the states of Washington and Alaska in the US, and is expanding to cover other areas. RLIN (Research Libraries Information Network) is a network supported by the Research Libraries Group (RLG) which comprises around twenty-five research libraries.

Outside the UK and the US, there are, of course, similar networks. UTLAS (University of Toronto Library Automation System) links over two hundred institutions, and although many of its users are in Canada, some are to be found as far afield as Japan. LIBRIS (Library Information System) is a major library automation project in Sweden.

Summary of the effects and benefits of computerization on cataloguing

Many of the changes in cataloguing practice and theory of the past fifteen years or so have been associated with the growing computerization of catalogue records and procedures. At first computers were seen as an aid in producing catalogues most effectively or efficiently, and this remains an important reason for computers being part of the cataloguing process. However, we are moving into the phase where information technology is starting to affect the form in which documents exist, and therefore the functions of the library service, and the records that a library must keep of its stock. The online public-access catalogue, for instance will in the future make it possible to re-assess the need for many traditional cataloguing practices. There is an awareness of the need for this re-assessment, but in practice this has not had, as yet, much effect on existing systems.

To concentrate, then, on the value of computers in improving the cataloguing process, many benefits have accrued from the opportunities that computers offer for shared databases and procedures. Briefly these can be summarized as:

a) The catalogue record has become the central bibliographic record for the library housekeeping system. These records can be used not only in the cataloguing subsystem, but also in other systems such as circulation control and acquisitions control. Conversely, this has made it necessary to consider the requirements of these systems when designing the form of the catalogue record.

b) Interchange of catalogue records has led to greater standardization in catalogue records. The tools which are used to support the creation of catalogue records, such as the Anglo-American Cataloguing Rules (First and Second Editions), the Dewey Decimal Classification Scheme, the Library of Congress Classification Scheme, and the International Standard Bibliographic Descriptions (ISBD's) have all been much more widely and much more literally adopted than was the case for their predecessors prior to the advent of computers. Further, these tools have become more important in the creation of effective catalogue records, and have themselves, in turn, been more closely refined than was necessary for their antecedents.

c) The availability of union catalogues in a more complete

form has been made for more effective inter-library lending, cooperative acquisitions policies and cooperative storage ventures, and other cooperative activities concerning library resources and their exploitation on a regional or national basis have become much more effective. Such a union catalogue record is an important prerequisite to the enhancement of document-delivery systems as discussed in chapter twelve.

d) No filing or other routine catalogue maintenance is required of cataloguers, except where it is necessary to alter stock records as the stock itself changes.

e) Different catalogue formats can be chosen for different catalogue locations, allowing both different record formats and differing physical forms of catalogues.

f) The relative cheapness and ease of printing copies of catalogues has made it possible to place both union and individual library system catalogues in a variety of locations.

g) The range of physical formats in which catalogues are to be encountered has altered drastically, and indeed may support very different search patterns from those possible in the traditional physical forms of catalogue.

h) Extracts from the main catalogue database may be printed or consulted online, so that the stock of a special collection or a branch may be identified.

i) The cataloguing procedure has become more structured, with a significant proportion of stock being processed quickly. The extent of shared cataloguing records has meant both shared expertise in cataloguing, but also a reduction in cataloguing effort, and therefore in the library resources which are devoted to cataloguing.

Further reading

Bakewell, K G B 'The UK library networks and the Co-operative Automation Group'. *Aslib proceedings* 34(6/7) June/July 1982. 301-9.

Boss, R W and Marcum, D B 'Online acquisitions systems for libraries'. *Library technology reports* 17(2) March/April 1981. 115-202.

Bryant, P 'Progress in documentation: the catalogue'. *Journal of documentation* 36(2) June 1980. 133-63.

Butcher, P 'Online acquisitions system at City University'. *Vine* 46 December 1982. 8-13.

Chapman, P 'Blaise Cortex: a microprocessor system for libraries'. *Information processing and management* 19(2) 1983. 77-81.

Malinconico, S M and Fasan, P J *The future of the catalog: the library's choices.* White Plains (New York), Knowledge Industry Publications, 1979.

Matthews, J R *Public access to online catalogs: a planning guide for managers.* Weston (C T), Online Inc, 1982.

Plaister, J *Computing in LASER: regional library co-operation.* London, LA, 1982.

Rowley, J 'Prospects for online public access catalogues' in *Proceedings of the 6th International Online Information Meeting, London, 7th-9th December 1982.* Oxford, Learned Information, 1982. 455-62.

Seal, A W *Automated cataloguing in the UK: a guide to services.* Bath, University Library, 1980. (BL R and D report 5545)

Seal, A W 'Online public access to library files in North America'. *Vine* 53 April 1984. 33-7.

Chapter Twelve

Circulation-control and document-delivery systems

All circulation-control and document-delivery systems impinge upon one of the primary functions of a library, document availability. Library materials, including books and non-book materials, should be made available to all customers immediately or as soon after the demand arises as is practicable. Circulation systems are more concerned with controlling stock within one library or library system. Document delivery is generally associated with the delivery of documents to users in their home location, or from a central store to local branch libraries, or between participating libraries in a network.

Principles of circulation control
In order to achieve maximum availability of material, all libraries must control circulation, by keeping, at the very least, records to specify:

what material is in the library stock or readily accessible through other channels;

which material is on loan, and from whom or where it can be retrieved;

when material on loan will next be available in the library for other customers.

Libraries differ in the priorities that they accord to each of these functions, depending to some extent on the level of demand that they experience and the urgency of the requests that they handle. Also, some groups of material and users may be differentiated; academic libraries, for instance, often operate short-term loan collections for student texts in great demand and offer differential loan periods to students and staff.

In addition to these three basic functions, most libraries

also like their circulation-control system to:

recognize and possibly trap reserved books on their return from loan;

prepare (including print and dispatch) overdue notices;

keep records of the number of books on loan to individual borrowers and notify overborrowing and dubious borrowers;

facilitate the calculation and collection of fines;

collect issue statistics;

be reliable;

be economic.

The implementation of computerized circulation systems started in the sixties. Early examples in the United Kingdom were West Sussex in the public library sector, Southampton University amongst academic libraries, and the Atomic Weapons Research Establishment in the special library sector. Now, many academic libraries in polytechnics and universities have such systems and many others are in the process of converting. Academic libraries are the most suitable candidates for computerization in this sphere, under current conditions, since they frequently have a few high-volume traffic points. If only a few service points need to be supported by the computer system, then only a few workstations are necessary in the computer system, and this reduces the investment and maintenance costs associated with the installation and maintenance of workstations. Hence, early developments of circulation-control systems in public libraries involved the installation of a computerized circulation system at the few larger or central libraries in the system, leaving the smaller branches with traditional card-based systems, or very rudimentary computer-based support (eg printed lists of transactions). With the increasing awareness of the potential of computerized circulation-control systems, and the improvement of telecommunications links, together with a greater willingness to finance the installation of workstations, public libraries are increasingly installing some form of computerized circulation-system in their branches, and even in mobile libraries. In special libraries and information units, computerized circulation control is more likely to be part of a more embracing package, which is likely to support other text-retrieval functions. Today, options exist which made it a realistic and economic proposition to consider computerized circulation control in almost any library or resource centre.

In considering the most suitable circulation-control system the following factors are important:

the number of items available for loan;

the number of items issued and returned every day, and the distribution of loans over time;

the number of reservations made daily;

the number of borrowers;

the number of branches and service points.

It is also important to attempt to anticipate any changes in the above parameters over the next few years. For a somewhat more embracing system it is also necessary to specify parameters relating to:

charging, renewals and overdues;

the number of charges and renewals daily;

the number of overdues;

the length of overdue notices, requests for return, notices of availability, etc.

Taken together these parameters will decide the basic characteristics of the computerized system, such as: the size of the processor, the number of terminals, the number of staff needed to operate the system, and whether telecommunications links are necessary and the nature of such links. Differing values of the above parameters lead to the wide variety of circulation-control systems, and so it is unlikely that one type of system will always be equally appropriate.

The first systems produced in the early to mid-1970s involved batch processing of the required records in the transactions file. Since the late-1970s, a number of online real-time circulation systems have emerged. These include turnkey systems from organizations such as GEAC, Plessey (now DS Ltd) and ALS, and the systems that have been developed by the cooperatives, such as OCLC and BLCMP. This leaves any library considering the implementation of a circulation-control system with three choices, the two options mentioned above, and the development of a local system. This option has been considered in general terms in chapter ten.

A survey of automated issue systems in (UK) public libraries provided an interesting summary of the installations that libraries in a particular sector were actually operating (as distinct from what was currently available in the market-place). This survey, conducted during 1983, reflected the fluidity of the situation. Many libraries were found to be considering changing or upgrading their system. This is perhaps related to the new features which are now available to libraries, but which are not being extensively exploited. For instance, although the trend towards stand-alone systems (with integration with other housekeeping functions) was clear, the survey showed that the majority of public libraries were still operating offline data-capture systems relying upon mainframe support.

Components of a computerized circulation-control system

Files

The core of the circulation-control system is the transactions or loans file. This file comprises a series of records, one for each transaction. Each record must, at the very least, specify:

> details of the document, eg book number;
> details of the borrower, eg borrower number;
> the date of the transaction (either the issue or return date).

Some systems maintain files which contain only records for items which are currently on loan. Such systems are known as 'transaction systems'. An alternative, which is becoming increasingly widespread, is the inventory control system. In such a system a permanent file of all possible loanable items is maintained with fields to indicate the location of the item, whether or not it is reserved, and to provide links to a book file. It is also possible to include some brief bibliographic details in these records, in order that such information is readily available when required for overdue or recall notices. Southampton University Library, for example, stores author, title and classmark.

It is common to keep bibliographical details in a separate book file. Without a book file, readers can only be notified of overdues, etc in terms of book numbers, which are likely to be meaningless to them. Many integrated systems rely upon the catalogue file to function as the book file because, in principle, there is no reason why this should not be a satisfactory arrangement. However, often the catalogue file is not entirely comprehensive and covers only recent stock. If a complete book file has to be built, this is a tiresome and time-consuming process. Another alternative is to create a sub-file of the catalogue or minicatalogue, which includes, for each book, say, author and title only.

A third file must contain more details of borrowers. In

printing overdues and making other contacts with borrowers it is essential to have the borrower's name and address. For statistical purposes it may be fruitful to know a little more about the borrower, such as his position, sex, educational background and age. Such details may often be transferred from another source, such as the university records or employment records.

Book and borrower numbers

The previous section made it clear that book and borrower numbers are an important component of the files and the input to the files of a circulation control system. Both book and borrower numbers must be assigned in such a way that they identify the book and the borrower uniquely.

Book numbers used in computerized circulation systems may be one of the following styles:

a) An accession number derived, usually, from an existing system of assigning accession numbers.

b) An alphabetic code or random number, which may often be assigned at random on the basis or pre-printed labels with numbers ready printed; such labels can easily be attached to books with little other preparation.

c) An ISBN-based book number. All ISBNs must be supplemented by a copy number, as ISBNs only uniquely identify a title and not the copy. The resulting number is rather needlessly lengthy. Also, many titles do not have ISBNs and it will be necessary to use a library equivalent to the ISBN for these titles.

d) A structured number which includes extra information about the copy. Many public libraries use non-ISBN systems based on nine- or ten-digit book numbers which specify: accession number, copy number and location. Often such numbers can be linked to ISBNs used heavily in catalogue systems.

The options for borrower numbers are similar, except that the ISBN or non-ISBN dilemma no longer pertains. Borrower numbers can take one of the following forms:

a) A ready-assigned number used throughout the organization, eg student number or employee code. The use of such a number contributes to the integration of all files on personnel.

b) A unique random number, which can be easy to assign.

c)   A structured number which carries information such as the branch at which the borrower is registered, and the borrower's status (eg resident, non-resident, student, etc).

Data collection and processing

Several data-collection devices and data-capture units have been evolved specifically for use in library circulation systems, although some of them also have other applications. These devices may constitute the inputting device in either a batch-processed or an online system. The trend is towards online processing, especially in systems currently being installed or developed.

Online systems permit the best control of stock. Issues can be recorded via a terminal and files immediately updated. Subsequent consultation of the files can be immediate and the files will communicate the current situation. Thus over-borrowing and problem borrowers can be identified at the circulation desk. Fines can be calculated on demand and reservations and other modifications to book records be made instantly or when time permits. Online systems usually have some back-up system to cover telecommunications or computer system failure. This back-up system will offer terminal recording showing various issue data, etc in an offline mode.

Apart from the added costs of an online system, one of the barriers to implementing an online approach is the cost and availability of computer time on a mainframe computer. The library may be constrained to use the local authority's or university's computer, which is unable to offer an adequate service throughout all library opening hours. A library-dedicated minicomputer is a great asset under such circumstances. A hybrid system involving both a minicomputer and a mainframe is a relatively common solution. The minicomputer typically validates and cumulates transactions, providing trapping stores and online access to the main loans file held on the mainframe computer. The mainframe updates the bibliographic details on the loans or transactions file and provides other back-up facilities.

Batch-processed systems necessarily rely on reams of print-out of transactions files etc. These print-outs are necessarily always out-of-date. A data-capture device transmits data to a punched paper tape or magnetic tape cassette. This is then dispatched and processed by the computer at intervals, of, say, twelve hours or daily, or weekly. Frequency of processing is conditioned by the computer centre constraints and the library's needs. Consultation of the issue file amounts to studying listings printed at the last processing, which do not, therefore, note recent loans. Reservations can likewise be checked on a further printed list. Overborrowing can only be traced by printing or interrogating the transactions file; and a file of fines and problem borrowers must be prepared in advance of the transaction. A trapping store is a useful aid. A trapping store holds book numbers and/or borrower numbers and indicates (by means of a light or buzz) when a reserved book or an unacceptable borrower passes through.

Data-capture devices

The most crude data-capture procedure involves the transcription or the details of the book and borrower on to pre-printed forms, by hand, at the issue desk (either by the reader or the library assistant). These may then be converted to machine-readable form, eg magnetic tape and input to the computer database. A slightly more sophisticated solution, which is likely to remain acceptable in libraries where the number of transactions is limited, is to type book and borrower details into the database via a terminal at the issue desk. This generally involves a little more effort at the issue stage than the other options outlined below, but avoids some of the problems of labelling of stock with special bar-coded labels, etc. The method is appropriate in some special libraries, school libraries and small college libraries.

Most libraries opt for special data-capture devices. These devices are designed to eliminate tiresome recording of details such as book number or title and borrower name each time that a book is processed. They, therefore speed up the process of recording issue transactions, and also are likely to result in more accurate records. The chief drawback of these methods is the requirement that every item of stock that is to be issued by the system must be appropriately labelled. The coding on the labels uniquely identifies a particular book, and is read by the data-capture device at the time of issue, etc in order to identify the book being loaned. Obviously the labelling of a large stock, such as that of a major university library, must be undertaken prior to the implementation of a circulation-control system, and constitutes a major task. Some of the better known special-purpose data-capture systems are: the ALS system, light pens and OCR.

The ALS system was based on coded book and borrower cards or labels. Their card-based system uses small punched cards, one per book and one per borrower. On issue both are placed in a reader and thus the book and the borrower can be identified and their identity recorded. The now more common label-based system relies on two non-magnetic metallic labels, each with a set of metallic dots. Both labels are passed over the sensing device on issue and data recorded on some machine-readable medium. (ALS data-collection terminals can also operate with a light pen attached, so that they can be used to read bar-coded labels.)

DS Ltd are known for their light-pen system which was designed for, and is widely used by, public libraries. Book and borrower numbers are encoded on labels as a bar code, ie a series of thick and thin lines. When a light-sensitive pen is passed over the label the pattern of lines is detected optically.

There are many ways of bar-coding information. In addition, for instance, to the original method adopted by DS Ltd, another well-known system is Telepen. Telepen was designed by SB Electronic Systems Ltd and incorporates a light pen and a teletypewriter. Telepen uses a flexible bar-code structure, which includes, for instance, alphabetic and numeric characters, and can operate with smaller and cheaper labels. A further method of bar-coding is that used by GEAC, known as Codabar. Many American libraries use Code-39 which includes alphabetic characters. Potential incompatibilities have been overcome by the ability of most of the suppliers to offer readers capable of reading other manufacturers' codes.

OCR readers have also been used in circulation-control systems. Here the reader recognizes OCR characters which have been typed onto a label. One label will be attached to each book and the same type of OCR characters will be found on borrower cards, etc.

All such data-capture devices form the basis of issue stations. Issue stations handle issues and discharges and possibly other functions, such as reservations. A large number of such stations may be linked to one system centre, which carries out checks and records data.

Considerations in selecting a data-collection device

Some systems offer options with regard to the data-collection device that may be used, others constrain users to exploit a particular type of device. Where a choice is available to a library there a number of factors that should be considered before a selection is made. Briefly these can be listed as:

a) Cost;

b) Environmental factors, eg is the equipment noisy? Is it comfortable and convenient for operators to use?

c) Labels, eg are they hard wearing? Can they be prepared in-house? Are they secure from user tampering?

d) Reliability, servicing and maintenance, eg is the equipment reliable? Are adequate arrangements possible for servicing and maintenance?

Examples of some circulation-control systems

Automated Library Systems Ltd (ALS)

ALS offers two systems one of which operates online (System 5) and the other offline (System 6). Both use the ALS bookreader which reads the labels in books and on borrower tickets to record the issue and return of books. The ALS bookreader also advises the operator of any trap relating to the book or borrower by the illumination of an appropriate panel. Data captured are either transmitted directly, in the case of System 5, or processed in batch mode from a magnetic medium. A barcode-reader may be used instead of the book-reader.

System 5 is a turnkey circulation-control system run on a dedicated minicomputer. All processing for the system, including production of overdue reminders, reports and the extraction of statistical data, is carried on the minicomputer, normally the SEL32, which is part of the systems centre. Processing of transaction data, including reservation and borrower traps, is carried out in real time, and online enquiries may be made to the short-entry catalogue and borrower details by means of a VDU supervisory station. ALS Browser terminals are a special-purpose terminal for enquiry purposes. Browser terminals have a tough-sensitive screen making them appropriate for public searching of the short-entry catalogue. Access to the catalogue via this screen is through author, title, author/title, classification number and control number. Back-up for the system, in case of line or system centre failure is provided by Line Protect Units, which record data onto floppy disk for later transmission to the system centre. Additional software packages are available to cover catalogue management and ordering and acquisitions.

System 6 provides a system of data capture with batch processing. The trapping store provides for the interception of reserved books and defaulting borrowers, and can be extended to indicate fines due, expired subscriptions, over-borrowing, etc. The VDU supervisory station is used to consult and modify the contents of the trapping store. The systems centre has two levels of capability, depending upon the size of the trapping store and the number of communication lines specified. Data are recorded onto magnetic tape or floppy disk or both for batch processing on a mainframe. There is an option of an interface with a central processor for transmitting data and remote loading of the trapping store. Line Protect Units provide back-up in the case of system centre failure, and, where data is recorded onto both tape and disk, the floppy disk is used to provide additional security. The systems centre can act as a standby recorder for System 5.

GEAC Computers Ltd
The GEAC library system is offered as a turnkey package on a dedicated minicomputer (GEAC 8000). Data for the circulation system are captured by light pens on terminals which read bar-code labels on books and borrower tickets. The bar code is Codabar, an American standard. The terminals provide function keys for the various routine tasks, such as issue, discharge and renewal, and can also be used for enquiries. Traps related to books and borrowers are signalled by display on the screen.

There are various options for the terminals. Those for circulation control and enquiry normally have 9 or 12-inch swivel screens, with or without light pens. There are also special terminals for public-access and data-entry purposes. Processing of transactions is carried out in real time. Book and borrower files may be accessed by various keys, including author, title, classification number, borrower name and number. Bibliographic data are held in variable-length fields defined by the library, and are compatible with MARC if so desired. The public-enquiry function has always been regarded as a special feature of the system, and this permits the public to search book files, to perform reservations, and to view information relating to their own transactions. Back-up for the system is provided by a back-up micro (a Commodore Pet). Data are captured onto floppy disk for later transmission to the 8000. Acquisitions and cataloguing packages are also available.

Plessey (now DS Ltd)
Over the years Plessey have marketed a number of systems. Those currently offered are the 7050 system, an offline data-capture system, Module 4, and online stand-alone system, and Module 3 which is an intermediate system between Module 4 and the 7050 system. Other systems which are no longer marketed but which are in common use are the Satellite system and the Stored Program Control system.

7050 system uses a microprocessor to control operations, but is essentially an offline data-capture system. Data are recorded onto magnetic tape for processing on the mainframe. Pens and composite terminals are used and there is a central teletype for inputting reservations and for printing out details of the reservations made. The trapping store is held on disk, giving a capacity of some 150,000 reservations. The disk also holds a copy of the day's transaction tape giving extra security. The trapping store can be interrogated using VDUs.

Module 3 offers the same facilities as the 7050 system, but also supports online transaction processing of a number-only stock file. In this option a full number-only file of the book-stock is available on disk (instead of a file relating only to reserved books). This file provides information including issue date, borrower number and renewal count, and allows for number enquiries via the VDU.

Module 4 is a turnkey circulation-control system run on a dedicated library machine. Processing is carried out in real time, and online enquiries by borrower, author, title and classification number may be made using the enquiry terminal. All processing for the system is carried out by a minicomputer, normally one of the Perkin-Elmer 3200 series, which performs background tasks while the circulation system is running, such as the generation of management-information reports and notices.

Edinburgh University Library

Edinburgh University library is in the process of implementing a system known as EULOGIA (Edinburgh University Library Online for General Information Access), which involves three inter-linked networks, and which will eventually suport:
 cataloguing;
 public catalogue enquiry;
 circulation (both short and normal loans);
 acquisition and ordering of books;
 serials management.

At the heart of the plan is the library's own system, based on a GEAC 8000 minicomputer located in the main library and with 60 enquiry terminals. This will carry the circulation system and the first-generation authoritative union catalogue of the library. All GEAC terminals will be located in the library

The GEAC computer is also a host on the University's network, and GEAC have developed the necessary interface to enable data to be transferred and read across the network. The University's network is based on two ICL 2900 main-frames, with a network of over 1,100 terminals, scattered across the campus. Direct lines extend to the Universities of Glasgow and Strathclyde, and a British Telecom gateway provides access to other individuals, networks and institutions.

Thus the library's catalogue data may be read and, where permitted, copied by internal and external users, provided that they are registered. In due course, it may be necessary to remove the catalogue database to a back-up host, so that the GEAC machine can handle circulation transactions at busy times.

The third element of the network is the SCOLCAP network based on a Hewlett Packard mainframe located in the National Library of Scotland. This will be used for online cataloguing and information sharing with other libraries, from about 1985.

This approach has been chosen in order to cater for a large, old, decentralized library system, with little previous implementation of computers.

Leicester University Library

The University of Leicester is a middle-sized, middle-aged institution and the library shows these characteristics, although it is comparatively well stocked for the size of the university. The stock is around three-quarters of a million volumes, and loans of 100,000 a year from the main collection and 300,000 a year from the large short-loan collection have to be covered by the circulation-control system.

The library is centralized on a single building, with the exception of the School of Education Library and the Clinical Sciences Library.

In 1979 a working party was formed to look into the possibility of computerizing the issue system for the short-loan collection. After some months' work in preparing a specification, suppliers were approached and possible systems examined. The only system which was likely to match the specification was SWALCAP. However, if SWALCAP was to be installed, the problem of gaining finance had to be negotiated. After investigating the cost-benefit of implementing various options it was decided to seek funding for a SWALCAP system to cover all loans and cataloguing.

In April 1981, the contract was signed with SWALCAP. The first decisions were associated with choosing from amongst the options offered by SWALCAP. The next step, once pre-printed bar-code labels had been chosen and ordered, was to process a trial batch ready to begin work at the end of July 1981.

In the short-loan collection there were 30,000 items to be bar-coded and entered in the bibliography file, the short-title file used by the circulation system. As much as possible was done before new readers arrived in October. Working entirely from the shelves, all books were recorded if they had a printed control number. These were recorded with the bar-code number and classmark for input to the SWALCAP cataloguing system as orders for MARC records to give, eventually, an automatically extracted bibliography file record. This procedure was fast, but did lead to some errors. Any remaining titles without control numbers had brief entries made individually by a cataloguer in the next six months. During Spring 1982 cabling was laid to support six light pens and six VDUs on the two issue counters. Next the external telecommunications link was installed, followed by the light pens and VDUs themselves.

In January 1983, 40,000 main library titles had been bar-coded and progress was satisfactory on bar-coding the complete stock.

Document-delivery systems

Obviously, as methods for reference retrieval improve so document-delivery systems must progress. It is of little value to be able to retrieve a reference and identify a useful docu-ment more quickly, if it still takes days to acquire the actual document. Currently most options offer supply of hard copy separate from the search and retrieval process. In order to speed things it is necessary to investigate means of:

either supplying hard copy ordered, during the search and retrieval process, or

supplying the full text as part of the retrieval process.

The latter of these options is achieved by the use of full-text databases, as introduced in chapter five. It is important to recognize that ultimately, full-text databases could, when they are sufficiently widely available, eliminate the need for other document-delivery systems.

Many of the more established document-delivery systems are offered by the online hosts. Strictly, these systems are document-ordering systems, since they only permit the user to transmit a request for a document to a third party, through the online host, and do not actually support the delivery of a document. Delivery is still by mail. SDC operates one such online document-ordering service known as Mail Drop.

Various experiments for improved document delivery systems are under way.

Project Hermes has been established during 1984 by the Department of Industry. The project is a teletex-based document-delivery service, which incorporates: document ordering, automatic document delivery, regular delivery of pre-specified documents, electronic mail, transfer of docu-ments between participants. It is intended that Hermes will also provide searching facilities, probably by links to existing database search systems. Delivery will be via telex, either immediately or overnight.

Note that HERMES uses teletex (not to be confused with Teletext). Teletex is an enhanced telex system. A teletex terminal is a device similar to a word processor.

The Adonis project aimed to supply facsimile images of pages from video disk. Adonis will use a combination of laser scanning/printing and digital optical storage of complete pages. Adonis was formed by a consortium, comprising Elsevier, Pergamon, Wiley, Academic, Springer and Blackwells Scientific, to provide the full text of their primary journals. Requests for copies would be sent to Adonis from the BLLD, thus reducing the effect of uncontrolled photocopying of journals. Elsevier is now the only publisher engaged in this project.

The EEC has funded research into an electronic document-delivery system, known as ARTEMIS. This will print out, at user's terminals, the pages of documents which have been requested after a search of an online database.

A group of Birmingham libraries, BCOP, has support from the British Library to install and monitor the value of facsimile-transmission machines in the libraries of its members, in the context of inter-lending. In the United States experiments with facsimile transmission in networks of libraries have been conducted by the Texas A & M University Consortium of Medical Libraries, and, separately, by the Smithsonian Institution libraries. Also a pilot project aimed at improving inter-library loan services in the Research Libraries Group with the aid of facsimile transmission is under way.

Further reading

'ALS integrated approach'. *Vine* 50 October 1983. 22-31.

Boss, R W and McQueen, J 'Automated circulation control systems'. *Library Technology Reports* 18(2) March/April 1982. 125-266.

Capewell, P and Morrison, K 'CIRCO live at Manchester Polytechnic library'. *Vine* 46 December 1982. 3-7.

Evans, M E 'University of York Library Automation Projects — developments'. *Program* 16(4) October 1982. 215-18.

Evans, M E 'University of York Library Automation Project: 1, the circulation system'. *Program* 13(2) April 1979. 85-95.

Evans, P W 'Barcodes, readers and printers for library applications'. *Program* 17(3) July 1983. 160-71.

Gratton, P D *Automation in Derbyshire County libraries*. London, Library Association, 1983.

Grose, M W 'Installing an automated system: SWALCAP at Leicester University'. *Vine* 47 March 1983.13-16.

Harrison, D J and Masters, B 'Progress with Plessey online at Kent County Libraries'. *Vine* 47 March 1983. 8-13.

Hawes, D F W and Botten, D A *Library automation at the Polytechnic of the South Bank*. London, Library Association, 1983. (Library Automation Case Studies).

Leaves, J 'Survey of automated issue systems in public libraries'. *Vine* 52 December 1983.

Line, M B 'Document delivery, now and in the future'. *Aslib Proceedings* 35(4) April 1983. 167-76.

Passmore, R B 'The use of computers in British public libraries: a survey'. *Program* 13(1) January 1979. 35-41.

Pickles, J S 'Input methods for United Kingdom computer-based circulation systems'. *Program* 11(2) April 1977. 47-63.

Rolling, S 'Chemical Abstracts' document delivery service'. *Online Review* 8(2) 1984. 183-91.

Wilson, C W J and Teskey, F N 'Harwell automated loans system − HAL using STATUS'. *Program* 15(2) April 1981. 43-65.

Yates, D M 'Project HERMES'. *Aslib Proceedings* 35(4) April 1983. 177-82.

Chapter Thirteen

Serials control

A serial, as defined by the International Serials Data System (ISDS), Paris is 'a publication issued in successive parts and intended to be continued indefinitely.' The definition continues: 'serials include periodicals, newspapers, annuals, journals, memoirs, proceedings, transactions etc of societies and monographic series. A serial can be in print or near print form and its parts usually have numerical or chronological designations.' Most libraries subscribe, at least in part to such a definition, but the term 'serial' is certainly not always used by all information workers to mean precisely the same categories of publications.

Serials are distinguished from monographs by their on-going nature. Any serials-control system usually has fewer titles to handle but must record more detail for each title and can expect a greater number of transactions per title. For this reason, amongst others, serials-control systems are often distinct from monograph systems, and address themselves uniquely to the problems posed by serials. An integrated serials-control system, nevertheless, features all three of the subsystems already encountered for monographs, viz:

1   ordering and acquisitions system — to control the selection, ordering, checking-in of serials, payment, and chasers when indexes or issues fail to arrive;

2   cataloguing—or keeping records of stock;

3   circulation control or keeping records of the availability of serials, to include circulation and binding.

It is also important to generate management statistics. It is not necessary to implement an integrated system which extends to all three major subsystems; one unit may operate satisfactorily in isolation. In fact, the majority of systems produce lists in various orders, eg by supplier, title or subject, and in a variety of different physical formats.

Problems unique to serials

In broad outline the ordering and cataloguing systems for serials have much in common with those for monographs. However, the following points summarize some of the features unique in serials control:

a) Successive issues are received at regular or irregular intervals, and it is important to ensure that successive issues arrive when they have been published (checking publication can cause difficulties);

b) Subscriptions must be renewed recurrently;

c) Catalogue data describe both the serial and the library's holdings of the serial and hence must be relatively extensive;

d) Serials change their titles, are published under variant titles (eg translated titles) and may change their frequency of publication. References must be inserted between associated periodicals and perodical titles;

e) The system should help with binding by holding and printing at the appropriate moment instructions for binding;

f) Serials may change their publisher;

g) Indexes, special issues and supplements must be controlled;

h) Some serials arrive, not by subscription, but, especially in special libraries and special collections, by gift or exchange.

A large amount of data must be held for each serial and frequent, repetitive record addition or amendment is necessary. For this reason alone, computerization is an attractive proposition for serials control. However, serials-control systems have been less influenced by cooperative and centralized practices, partly due to their academic and special library context. Hence serials-control systems are more likely to be unique, than parallel systems for monographs.

Development of computerized serials-control systems has lagged behind similar systems for monographs. This slower progress has in part been due to the essential complexity of a complete serials-control system, but also derives from the lower priority associated with serials-control as compared with monographs control. More development of serials-control systems has been undertaken in academic and special libraries where serials represent a larger proportion of the stock, than in, say, public lending libraries.

Today the majority of computerized serials-control systems remain batch processed, on a mainframe computer, and are used primarily to produce lists of serials. There are more advanced online, real-time, integrated serials-control systems, but many of these have not yet made a significant impact on record-keeping in individual libraries. Services have been, or are being, developed and implemented by the library cooperatives, special subscription agencies and some other organizations, such as the producers of text-retrieval software. After a discussion of the principles of serials control, this chapter will describe some systems which have made a contribution to serials control.

Serials control subsystems

Ordering and acquisitions systems

The initial ordering of a serial is akin to ordering a book. Ordering must encompass processes for requesting, approving, checking, ordering and accounting, in respect of each new serial title.

The chief difficulties arise with the continuing nature of the subscriptions to serials. Renewals must be created and dispatched at the appropriate time. Hence, the ordering must contain records of renewal dates and subscription levels and processing must include the capacity for scanning records to check for renewal dates. Further, sufficient data to facilitate the identification of the vendor or society, from whom the serial is to be ordered, must be included.

As issues appear regularly, acquisitions is one of the major functions in any serials-control system. The acquisitions function may be divided into receiving and claiming. Receiving involves a large volume of checking. When an issue arrives it must be checked to ensure that it is the correct item and then the master records must be amended to reflect new receipts. As the arrival of each issue must be noted, several attempts have been made to reduce this workload. Typically, for instance, a file of punched cards may be created of all serials to be received. When the issue arrives the card file is searched and extracted, and a card created if no appropriate card is present in the file. All cards corresponding to received issues are eventually processed in a batch and the computer-held master file updated. Any remaining cards serve to alert the librarian to the non-arrival of certain issues. Alternatives to this routine include marking issues received on a check-list and online data entry as the issue is received.

The claiming function is a smaller, but possibly more complex activity. The point at which claiming procedures are to be initiated must be a matter for the professional judgement of the librarian. The computer can help by providing lists of the information that the librarian needs in order to exercise this judgement.

A further function also linked to the accessions function is subscriptions control. In order to fulfil this function, the master record must include details of when the subscriptions are to be renewed. At regular intervals, a list of subscriptions ripe for renewal is printed for the librarian's perusal. After a decision on renewal has been made, computer-printed renewal notices may be generated. The other responsibility of the computer in this context is likely to be the keeping of accounts and printing them when necessary. These printed lists of the financial situation are a useful management tool and make it easier to keep the level of subscriptions under review.

Cataloguing systems

Catalogue formats, orders, processes, etc are fundamentally similar for serials or monographs. From the master file, listings can be generated in several orders, eg title, subject, location, supplier. Serials catalogues may be printed in book-form or microform and general or selective listings are possible. The frequency of update of such listings varies, but usually lies between the limits defined by monthly and annually. Union lists are known, such as the lists for Essex County Libraries, and BLCMP.

The content and format of the serial bibliographic record varies considerably between systems. Some catalogues are based on ISBD(S) and others ISDS formats, whilst other systems use local formats. One problem that all cataloguers must address themselves to is that of changed and variant titles. References must be provided between linked titles.

Circulation control and binding

Circulation, with respect to serials, frequently adopts different patterns from those obtaining for books. If serials are available for ordinary loan, then the same circulation-control system will suffice as for monographs. Often, however, serials are reserved for reference use only. In special libraries, special circulation systems are common and if these are large enough, they may be computerized. Specific journals are circulated to those readers who have expressed an interest in that title. A computerized system to control this activity must have a list of serials taken, a list of users and their addresses and some indication of the serials to be directed towards specific users. The computer can then be expected to print a list of readers, that can be appended to each issue of each title.

Files
In order to perform the above functions, the serials-control system must have a number of core files. The entire system hinges on the master serials records file. This file includes master serial data records; each record in an embracing serials system will include:

1   cataloguing data—the records may be MARC-based, or simple fixed field;

2   ordering data, including renewal dates, names and addresses of publisher, code for vendor, costs;

3   receiving data, such as frequency of publication, irregularities, claiming criteria;

4   binding data, such as colour and style of binding, number of issues per binding volume, type of binding;

5   holdings data;

6   circulation data, ie names and addresses of locations for circulation.

Such data may form the basis of a set of lists, which aid in the control of the various functions. Such lists might cover receiving records, invoice control, bindery control, error list, claims and renewal requests, new accessions list, holdings list and statistical summaries.

Some serials-control systems

International Serials Data System
Set up in 1972, the International Serials Data System (ISDS), was initiated by the Unesco member states under the umbrella of UNISIST. The International Centre (IC) was set up in 1972 in Paris, with four main functions:

Management information
↓
Selection for purchase
↓
Ordering (including renewals of subscriptions)
↓
Receiving issues and claiming for issues not received
↓
Recording current holdings and allowing access to lists of such
↓
Circulation of issues and borrowing
↓
Binding

Figure 13.1: Functions to be covered by a serials-control system

1   to create an international file of serial publications; all serials entered in this file are assigned an ISSN;

2   to assign an ISSN to each new serial, and promote their use;

3   to establish a communications network between libraries, secondary information services, publishers of serial literature and international organizations;

4   to promote international standards for bibliographic description, communication formats and information exchange, in the area of serials publishing and control.

The ISSN (International Standard Serial Number) is a seven-digit (plus one check digit) code with no meaning. Since the numbers are simply sequential the system is hospitable to all serials, dead or alive.

Around 45 national centres have been established in Europe, Japan, United States of America, USSR, including the National Serials Data Centre in the United Kingdom. These centres register and allocate ISSNs. Their other functions include:

1   to aid libraries involved in computerization of serials-catalogue records by providing machine-readable serials records;

2   to form an access point to an international network of serials publications;

3   to develop a computer-based information service on the holdings of serials across their country.

The basic file is maintained by the IC by merging the files of serials titles. Details of the registration of new and changed titles are sent from the national centres to the IC where they are added to the ISDS register and announced in the *ISDS Bulletin*. The main file contains 200,000 records with 25 to 30,000 records being added each year. Machine-readable versions of this file or subsets of it are available, or sets of the records can be purchased on COM fiche.

ISDS records can be used in computer-based library catalogues, since they contain minimal, but sufficient, information. As they are available in the MARC exchange format the records are potentially accessible from a variety of access points. The object of the ISDS records is to give sufficient identification for the unique allocation of ISSNs. The ISDS consider that the following components are adequate for this purpose:

key title
abbreviated title
variant title(s)
imprint
former title(s)
successor title(s)
other language edition of
has other language edition(s)
inset or supplement to
has inset or supplement
related title(s).

A fuller record may be achieved by using the International Standard Bibliographic Description for Serials (ISBD(S)). The intention of this standard is to define the elements necessary to describe a serial bibliographically and to determine their order and the punctuation to be inserted between them. Such records from different sources should then be interchangeable and contribute to the conversion of bibliographic records to machine-readable form. In broad outline the ISBD(S) falls within the framework of the ISBD(G), the general framework for bibliographic description.

CONSER

CONSER is a major North-American project which contributes towards the maintenance of serials records. CONSER (Conversion of Serials) was approved in 1973, and the US

Council on Library Resources sponsored the project, with the Library of Congress and the National Library of Canada authenticating the serials records which were created. The database was built upon the Minnesota Union List of Serials (MULS) together with the LC and National Library of Canada MARC records for serials, the records of the Pittsburgh Regional Library Center, and those of the US National Agricultural Library and the National Library of Medicine. The database was created and maintained on the OCLC host computer, and by 1977 OCLC had assumed managerial responsibility for the project. There are now around twenty libraries participating in the project and over 130,000 records have been included. CONSER records may be used in union lists, bibliographies, information retrieval and as a basis for selection and acquisition. Products available from CONSER include: a) weekly tapes of serials records; b) a Keyword-out-of-context index of serials titles; and c) a microfiche of authenticated records.

Subscription agency services

Many of the serials subscription agencies have begun to offer libraries services which support libraries in their serials-control activities. These services have emerged from the agencies' in-house systems for ordering, claiming and supplying serials. These can cover:

1   *Subscription handling* is plainly the basic service that these agencies have always offered, but it is now offered as a computerized system, to cover contacting publishers concerning rates, ordering, preparing invoices and dealing with renewals.

2   *Bibliographic information relating to serials:* This is an easy-to-produce by-product of the subscription-handling services, but the quality of the bibliographic information on offer does vary. The information may be available in a variety of physical formats including microforms and online access.

3   *Accounting and management information* including detailed expenditure figures for serials, organized by account, budget code, subject, etc.

4   *Issue receiving.*

5   *Production of union lists.*

Blackwell's, UK

Blackwell's is probably the largest UK-based serials subscription agency, and as such has found it appropriate to develop computerized support services, in the form of PERLINE. PERLINE'S main functions are available to all customers, who can get access to files on the host computer via tele-type terminals. These functions are:

a) File interrogation, so that the user may search for details of serials and examine subscriptions records;

b) Customized news bulletins, which cover items of news relevant to a particular customer, such as changes in titles, publishers' replies to claims;

c) Generation of claims.

PEARL (Periodicals Enquiry Acquisition and Registration Locally) is a software package which can be run on a small computer, such as Digital's PDP/11/23, in the local library, and hold many of the library's own files locally. This package allows the user to interact with Blackwell's mainframe computer, but this is only necessary when some action is to be communicated to outsiders, such as the placing of orders. PEARL operates with seven files. These cover: serial titles, patrons, orders, circulation, suppliers, publishers and funds. With the use of these files it is possible to perform the following functions:

a) Check-in of issues;

b) Claiming of issues not received;

c) Sending messages to Blackwell's mainframe;

d) Fund accounting;

e) Ordering new titles;

f) Maintenance of serial, patron, supplier and publisher files.

Retrieval of records is via the ISSN, ISBN (for monographic series), CODEN and words in the title.

PERLINE at UKAEA, Risley

The United Kingdom Atomic Energy Authority library at Risley has an early implementation of PERLINE, which makes use of PEARL. This installation does not exploit all of the features of PERLINE, but does demonstrate how the facilities available may be tailored to a specific application.

The library serves a site of 18 buildings, with a population of 4,500, subscribes to 1,000 titles and has 750 users on periodical circulation lists. In addition there are significant monograph and report collections. The library sought a package which would encompass all aspects of its housekeeping.

At the time when the library started to cast around for a computerized housekeeping system, Blackwell's handled 90% of the library's serials subscriptions and 70% of the book orders. PERLINE was chosen because Blackwell's offered a high level of support and training, and had a good appreciation of library operations and problems. The implementation of PERLINE will be followed by the introduction of BOOKLINE/AMBER, for monographs, in the near future.

The local database runs on a DEC LSI-11/23 with 128 Kb memory and a 20 Mb Winchester disk. Other equipment includes a cartridge for copying to back-up tapes, 2 VT 101 terminals, a MT4201 printer, a synchronous data port and 2 synchronous line drivers, and a modem for access to Blackwell's file.

Database creation was a potential problem area, but this was in fact readily overcome, since Blackwells already had records for 90% of the periodicals held at Risley. The records for the remaining titles were input online locally. The local systems works on a series of interconnected interactive files, covering serials, patrons, suppliers, publishers, orders, circulation records, and holdings respectively. The serial file is maintained in alphabetical order and holds details of title, alternative title(s), ISSN, notes, subscriptions, supplier, publisher, and holdings. Supplier and publisher details can be input by code and are maintained in full in their respective files. The holdings file stores for each issue the date published, date expected, date received, quantity received and the status (eg arrived, predicted, etc).

Prediction of the expected arrival date of periodical issues can be performed on the basis of an examination of holdings data, such as the date published, the date expected and the date recorded, over a period of time. Data for each expected issue can be modified according to an analysis of previous patterns (after an initial phase).

The patron or borrower file had to be created locally, and contains: name, initials, title, ID, two addresses, coded field of subject interest and two fields for circulation of items. A weighting factor can be applied to indicate priority on a distribution list, and there is a facility to suspend a patron from all circulation lists until a specified date (to cover, for instance, leaves or absences).

The enquiry subsystem is menu-driven. The initial master menu offers sixteen choices, one of which may be selected by the input of three-character alphabetical codes. Further menus allow the user to perform other functions, eg display, amend, delete. Enquiries can be performed through the following access points for the serials file: title, abbreviated title, ISSN and CODEN, and through the following points for the patron file: patron number, surname and first initial or truncated surname. This file will show all of the periodicals that are circulated to a patron and how they are received.

Serials, as they arrive, are usually checked-in by keying in the abbreviated title. The system responds with details of the last issue received and the number of library copies expected. The user is then prompted for the input of issue details and the number of copies received. If these are accepted, the operator can amend circulation lists temporarily, and then circulation lists can be printed either individually or as a batch. Where there is a shortage of delivery (ie insufficient copies received), the operator can write that issue to a claims file for review.

A further routine permits the recording of the return of each issue after circulation, and although some modifications were necessary to make this successful in this application, this is now operating successfully.

Loughborough University of Technology

Loughborough University of Technology has developed MINICS (Minimal Input Cataloguing System) which covers both serials and monographs. MINICS records are locally created records in a simplified MARC-type structure; the records are simpler than MARC records. More specifically MINICS aims to:

a) cover serials/series-level entries, monographic or item-level ones and analyticals or 'item within' via the same file format.

b) cover any publication medium with the same format.

c) be compatible with MARC records, yet retain a simpler format.

d) exploit the advantages of a variable length format.

e) avoid duplication of data at input by using programs that piece together and interlink the contents of records.

f) make the catalogue master file serve as an accessions

archive and use the same format for an information-retrieval system.

g) allow flexibility in the nature of the catalogue to permit union listing, etc.

h) interface with other subsystems, such as orders, serials financial control, serials corporate author file and serials automated accession.

Online input and editing for each cataloguer and an online accessioning system, together with an online in-process file of orders and items received, are planned as features of MINICS for the near future.

A system which pre-dated MINICS is another locally produced system, PDS; PDS is a fixed-field system which is still used locally alongside MINICS at Loughborough University. This has also become the basis for an area academic libraries union list of serials, involving the universities of Loughborough, Leicester and Nottingham.

A feature of all Loughborough University's systems is that they have been designed independently of cooperatives, and are designed locally to suit a local specification.

Loughborough University was also a partner in the project to produce MASS (MARC-based Automated Serials System). Developed in cooperation with BLCMP, and linked to MINICS, MASS has three aims:

1   To provide data-element compatibility with the MARC serials format, thereby allowing the sharing of data to produce national or area union lists, as well as individual library holdings lists or subject indexes.

2   To record information of local utility, such as binding, ordering subscriptions and similar data.

3   To allow maximum flexibility to suit other libraries.

Further reading

Anderson, D 'Compatibility of ISDS and ISBD(S) records in international exchange: the background'. *International cataloguing* 12(2) 1983. 14-17.

Birmingham Libraries Cooperative Mechanization Project *BLCMP MASS Manual: input procedures for serials cataloguing* Birmingham, BLCMP, 1973.

Bourne, R 'Building a serials file'. *Program* 12(2) 1978. 78-86.

Bourne, R (ed) *Serials librarianship.* London, LA, 1980.

Graham, F 'PERLINE at Risley: online serials control in a special library'. *Vine* 49 August 1983. 30-1.

Graham, M E (ed) *Automation and serials: proceedings of the UK Serials Group Conference, Cardiff, 1980.* Loughborough, UK Serials Group, 1981.

Harley, A J 'Automated serials control at the British Library Lending Division'. *Program* 15(4) October 1981. 200-8.

Iijama, M and Ono, S 'Online serials control in library management' in *Proceedings of the 6th International Online Information Meeting, London, 7th-9th December 1982* Oxford, Learned Information, 1983, 415-31.

Marks, T 'PERLINE at Risley'. *Information technology and libraries* 2(1) March 1983, 56-7.

Rodgers, L J 'The University of London's union list of serials'. *Aslib proceedings* 34(4) April 1982. 193-7.

Sauer, M 'Automated serials control: cataloguing considerations'. *Journal of Library Automation* 9(1), March 1976, 8-18.

Shaw, D F 'Serials control'. *Aslib proceedings* 34(2) February 1982. 81-9.

Szilvassy, J 'ISDS: worldwide serials control'. *IFLA Journal* 8(4) 1982. 371-7.

Walbridge, S 'CONSER and OCLC'. *Serials review* 6(3) July/September 1980. 109-11.

Index

Filing is letter by letter, treating abbreviations as words. Concepts which are treated at some length are indexed, but individual databases, hosts, programming languages etc are not listed in the index when they are only cited in the text as examples. In most instances, where it seemed helpful to do so, abbreviations have been entered in addition to the full version of the term or name.